The Original
Summer Bridge Activities™

Bridging Grades Prekindergarten to Kindergarten

MW00700296

We're so glad you decided to join us on a fun-filled summer learning adventure. Be sure to access your **FREE Summer Bridge Activities™** online companion.

Here's how:

Step 1: Visit **www.summerlearningactivities.com/sba**

Step 2: Register your **Summer Bridge Activities™** book

Step 3: Download the **FREE Summer Bridge Activities™** mobile apps

Summer Bridge Activities™
online companion

Welcome,   My account settings   **Log out**

Welcome to Summer Bridge Activities! We're so glad you decided to join us on a fun-filled summer learning adventure. To get the most out of your online companion click here for tips and frequently asked questions.

| **Child 1** | **Add Child ➕** |

Child 1   Update Child's Password

Bridging Grades PK to K

Assessments

Focused Practice Workbooks

Incentive Contracts

Family Fun

Mobile Apps

Preview Games

Caution: Exercise activities may require adult supervision. Before beginning any exercise activity, consult a physician. Written parental permission is suggested for those using this book in group situations. Children should always warm up prior to beginning any exercise activity and should stop immediately if they feel any discomfort during exercise.

Caution: Before beginning any food activity, ask parents' permission and inquire about the child's food allergies and religious or other food restrictions.

Caution: Nature activities may require adult supervision. Before beginning any nature activity, ask parents' permission and inquire about the child's plant and animal allergies. Remind the child not to touch plants or animals during the activity without adult supervision.

The authors and publisher are not responsible or liable for any injury that may result from performing the exercises or activities in this book.

Credits

Series Creator: Michele D. Van Leeuwen

Content Editor: JulieAnna Kirsch

Copy Editor: Barrie Hoople

Layout and Cover Design: Chasity Rice

Cover Art: Robbie Short

© 2010, Carson-Dellosa Publishing Company, Inc., PO Box 35665, Greensboro, North Carolina 27425. The purchase of this material entitles the buyer to reproduce worksheets and activities for classroom use only—not for commercial resale. Reproduction of these materials for an entire school or district is prohibited. No part of this book may be reproduced (except as noted above), stored in a retrieval system, or transmitted in any form or by any means (mechanically, electronically, recording, etc.) without the prior written consent of Carson-Dellosa Publishing Co., Inc.

Printed in the USA • All rights reserved.

ISBN 978-1-60418-817-2
03-128121151

Table of Contents

© Carson-Dellosa

About Summer Learning

Dear Parents:

Did you know that many children experience learning loss when they do not engage in educational activities during the summer? This means that some of what they have spent time learning over the preceding school year evaporates during the summer months. However, summer learning loss is something that you can help prevent. Below are a few suggestions for fun and engaging activities that can help children maintain and grow their academic skills during the summer.

- Read with your child every day. Visit your local library together and select books on subjects that interest your child.

- Ask your child's teacher to recommend books for summer reading.

- Explore parks, nature preserves, museums, and cultural centers.

- Consider every day as a day full of teachable moments. Measuring ingredients for recipes and reviewing maps before a car trip are ways to learn or reinforce skills.

- Each day, set goals for your child to accomplish. For example, complete five math problems or read one section or chapter in a book.

- Encourage your child to complete the activities in books such as Summer Bridge Activities™ to help bridge the summer learning gap.

To learn more about summer learning loss and summer learning programs, visit *www.summerlearning.org.*

Have a memorable summer!

Brenda McLaughlin and Sarah Pitcock
National Summer Learning Association

© Carson-Dellosa

About Summer Bridge Activities™

Prepare your child for kindergarten with *Summer Bridge Activities™: Bridging Grades Prekindergarten to Kindergarten*! The activities in this book are designed to review the skills that your child mastered in prekindergarten, preview the skills that he or she will learn in kindergarten, and help prevent summer learning loss. No matter how wonderful your child's classroom experiences are, your involvement outside of the classroom is crucial to his or her academic success. Together with *Summer Bridge Activities™: Bridging Grades Prekindergarten to Kindergarten*, you can fill the summer months with learning experiences that will deepen and enrich your child's knowledge and prepare him or her for the upcoming school year.

Summer Bridge Activities™ is the original workbook series developed to help parents support their children academically during the summer months. While many other summer workbook series are available, Summer Bridge Activities™ continues to be the series that teachers recommend most.

The three sections in this workbook correspond to the three months of traditional summer vacation. Each section begins with a goal-setting activity, a word list, and information for parents about the fitness and character development activities located throughout the section.

To achieve maximum results, your child should complete two activity pages each day. Activities cover a range of subjects, including beginning phonics, numbers and counting, handwriting, fine motor skills, and shapes and colors. These age-appropriate activities are presented in a fun and creative way to challenge and engage your child. Each activity page is numbered by day, and each day includes a space for your child to place a colorful, motivational sticker after he or she completes the day's activities.

Bonus science experiments, fitness and character development exercises, and extension activities that encourage outdoor learning are located at the end of each section. Complete these activities with your child throughout each month as time allows.

A bonus phonics and handwriting section at the end of the book provides extra practice on these important kindergarten skills. The included flash cards reinforce basic skills, and a certificate of completion will help you and your child celebrate summer learning success!

© Carson-Dellosa

Skills Matrix

Day	Alphabet	Character Development	Classification	Colors	Fine Motor Skills	Fitness	Handwriting	Measurement	Numbers & Counting	Patterning	Phonics	Science	Sequencing	Shape Recognition	Visual Discrimination
1								★							★
2					★									★	
3					★									★	
4					★									★	
5					★									★	
6					★									★	
7					★				★						
8									★					★	
9				★					★					★	
10									★					★	
11									★						
12									★						★
13									★						★
14									★						
15									★						
16									★						
17				★	★				★					★	
18									★						★
19					★										★
20					★										★
BONUS	★	★			★	★			★			★		★	
1									★						
2				★					★						
3				★			★				★				
4				★			★				★				
5				★			★				★				
6				★			★				★				
7				★			★				★				
8				★			★				★				
9				★			★				★				
10							★		★		★				
11							★		★		★				

© Carson-Dellosa

Skills Matrix

Day	Alphabet	Character Development	Classification	Colors	Fine Motor Skills	Fitness	Handwriting	Measurement	Numbers & Counting	Patterning	Phonics	Science	Sequencing	Shape Recognition	Visual Discrimination
12				★			★				★				
13							★				★				
14				★			★		★		★				
15							★		★		★				
16							★			★	★				
17					★		★				★			★	
18			★				★				★				
19							★				★				★
20							★				★				★
BONUS	★	★	★		★	★						★			
1			★				★				★				
2							★				★				★
3							★				★				★
4							★				★				
5							★				★				
6							★		★		★				
7							★		★		★			★	
8					★		★		★		★				
9	★						★								
10			★	★											
11			★												
12													★		
13					★										★
14											★				
15											★				
16											★				
17											★				
18											★				
19											★				
20								★			★				
BONUS		★	★			★	★		★		★	★			

© Carson-Dellosa

Encouraging Summer Reading

Literacy is the single most important skill that your child needs to be successful in school. The following list includes ideas of ways that you can help your child discover the great adventures of reading!

- Establish a time for reading each day. Ask your child about what he or she is reading. Try to relate the material to an event that is happening this summer or to another book or story.

- Let your child see you reading for enjoyment. Talk about the great things that you discover when you read.

- Create a summer reading list. Choose books from the reading list (pages ix–x) or head to the library and explore the shelves. A general rule for selecting books at the appropriate reading level is to choose a page and ask your child to read it aloud. If he or she does not know more than five words on the page, the book may be too difficult.

- Read newspaper and magazine articles, recipes, menus, maps, and street signs on a daily basis to show your child the importance of reading.

- Find books that relate to your child's experiences. For example, if you are going camping, find a book about camping. This will help your child develop new interests.

- Visit the library each week. Let your child choose his or her own books, but do not hesitate to ask your librarian for suggestions. Often, librarians can recommend books based on what your child enjoyed in the past.

- Make up stories. This is especially fun to do in the car, on camping trips, or while waiting at the airport. Encourage your child to tell a story with a beginning, a middle, and an end. Or, have your child start a story and let other family members build on it.

- Encourage your child to join a summer reading club at the library or a local bookstore. Your child may enjoy talking to other children about the books that he or she has read.

© Carson-Dellosa

Summer Reading List

The summer reading list includes fiction and nonfiction titles. Experts recommend that parents read to prekindergarten and kindergarten children for at least 10 minutes each day and ask questions about the story to reinforce comprehension.

Decide on an amount of daily reading time for each month. You may want to write the time on each monthly goal page at the beginning of each section.

Fiction

Barrett, Judi
Cloudy with a Chance of Meatballs

Bemelmans, Ludwig
Madeline

Boynton, Sandra
Moo, Baa, La La La!

Brett, Jan
Goldilocks and the Three Bears

Bridwell, Norman
Clifford, the Big Red Dog

Brown, Margaret Wise
Goodnight Moon

Carle, Eric
Brown Bear, Brown Bear, What Do You See?
The Grouchy Ladybug
The Very Hungry Caterpillar

Cronin, Doreen
Thump, Quack, Moo: A Whacky Adventure

Feiffer, Jules
Bark, George

Freeman, Don
Corduroy

Guarino, Deborah
Is Your Mama a Llama?

Henkes, Kevin
Kitten's First Full Moon

Johnson, Crockett
Harold and the Purple Crayon

Keats, Ezra Jack
The Snowy Day

Lies, Brian
Bats at the Library

Long, Melinda
How I Became a Pirate

Mayer, Mercer
There's a Nightmare in My Closet

McCloskey, Robert
Make Way for Ducklings

Numeroff, Laura
If You Give a Cat a Cupcake
If You Give a Mouse a Cookie

© Carson-Dellosa

Summer Reading List (continued)

Fiction (continued)

Portis, Antoinette
Not a Box

Potter, Beatrix
The Tale of Peter Rabbit

Rey, H. A.
Curious George

Rosenthal, Amy Krouse
Little Pea

Seuss, Dr.
The Cat in the Hat
Horton Hears a Who!
The Lorax

Shaw, Nancy
Sheep in a Jeep

Trivizas, Eugene
*The Three Little Wolves and the
    Big Bad Pig*

Ward, Michael
Mike and the Bike

Wiesner, David
Flotsom

Willems, Mo
Don't Let the Pigeon Drive the Bus!
The Pigeon Finds a Hot Dog!

Nonfiction

Anno, Mitsumasa
Anno's Counting Book

Aston, Dianna Hutts
A Seed Is Sleepy

Ehlert, Lois
*Eating the Alphabet: Fruits &
    Vegetables from A to Z*
Leaf Man

Heiligman, Deborah
From Caterpillar to Butterfly

Jenkins, Steve
Actual Size

Mortenson, Greg
*Listen to the Wind: The Story of Dr. Greg
    and "Three Cups of Tea"*

Page, Robin
What Do You Do with a Tail Like This?

Sabuda, Robert
*Encyclopedia Prehistorica Dinosaurs: The
    Definitive Pop-Up!*

© Carson-Dellosa

Monthly Goals

A *goal* is something that you want to accomplish. Sometimes, reaching a goal can be hard work!

Think of three goals that you would like to set for yourself this month. For example, you may want to exercise for 10 minutes each day. Have an adult help you write your goals on the lines.

Place a sticker next to each goal you complete. Feel proud that you have met your goals!

1. _____ PLACE STICKER HERE

2. _____ PLACE STICKER HERE

3. _____ PLACE STICKER HERE

Word List

The following words are used in this section. They are good words for you to know. Read each word aloud with an adult. When you see a word from this list on a page, circle it with your favorite color of crayon.

big	little
circle	same
color	shape
count	trace
draw	write

© Carson-Dellosa

Introduction to Flexibility

At the end of this section are fitness and character development activities that focus on flexibility. These activities are designed to get your child moving and thinking about building her physical fitness and her character. Complete these activities throughout the month as time allows.

Physical Flexibility

Flexibility is usually understood to mean the ability to accomplish everyday tasks easily, like bending to tie a shoe. These everyday tasks can be difficult for people whose muscles and joints have not been used and stretched regularly.

Proper stretching allows muscles and joints to move through their full range of motion, which is key to maintaining good flexibility. There are many ways that your child stretches every day without realizing it. She may reach for a dropped pencil or a box of cereal. Point out these examples to your child and explain why good flexibility is important to her health and growth. Challenge her to improve her flexibility consciously. Encourage her to set a stretching goal for the summer, such as practicing daily until she can touch her toes.

Flexibility of Character

While it is important to have a flexible body, it is also important to be mentally flexible. Share with your child that being mentally flexible means being open-minded to change. Talk about how disappointing it can be when things do not go her way and that this is a normal reaction. Give a recent example of when unforeseen circumstances ruined her plans, such as having a trip to the park canceled because of rain. Explain that there will be situations in life where unexpected things happen. Often, it is how a person reacts to those circumstances that affects the desirability of the outcome. By using examples your child can relate to, you can arm her with the tools to be flexible, such as having realistic expectations, brainstorming solutions to improve a disappointing situation, and looking for good things that may have resulted from the initial disappointment.

Inner flexibility can take many forms. For example, respecting the differences of other children, sharing, and taking turns are ways that a child can practice flexibility. Encourage your child to be flexible and praise her when you see her exhibiting this important character trait.

© Carson-Dellosa

Track your growth this summer. Have an adult help you measure your height and weight. Fill in the blanks. Then, draw yourself below and color the picture.

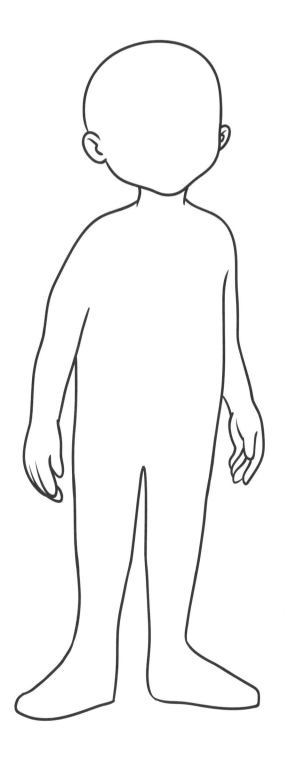

Your Height:

_____

Your Weight:

_____

© Carson-Dellosa

DAY 1

Circle the picture in each row that is the same as the first picture.

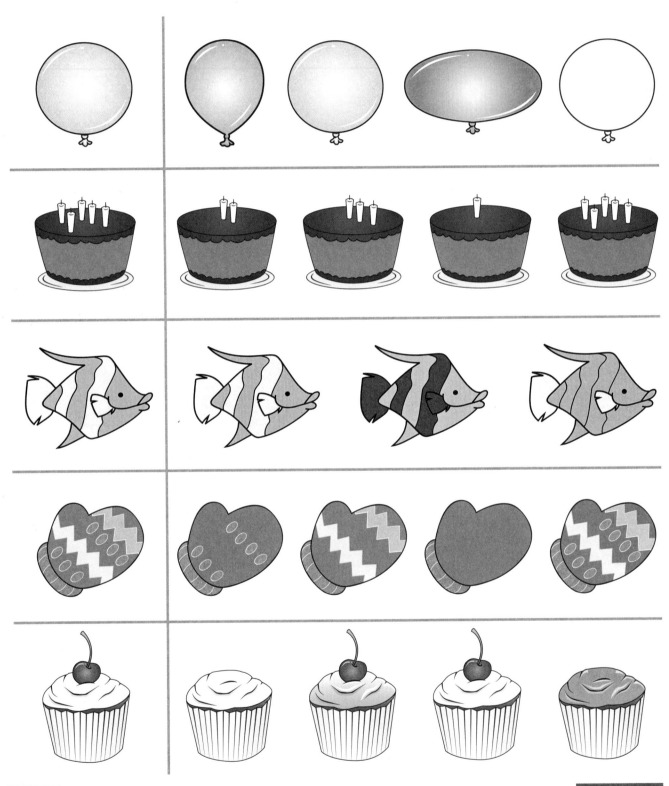

© Carson-Dellosa

PLACE
STICKER
HERE

Trace the dashed lines.

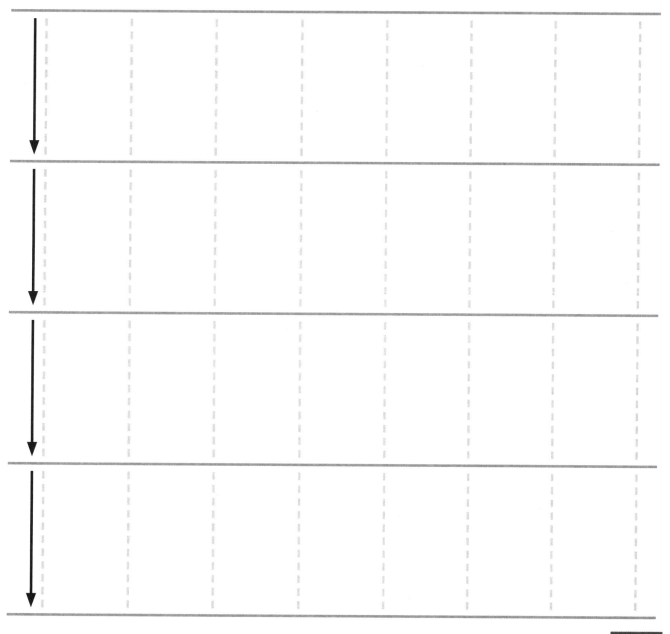

© Carson-Dellosa

DAY 2

This is a square.

Color the squares.

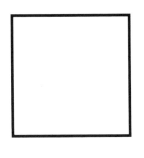
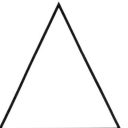
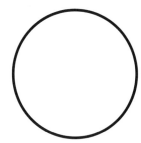
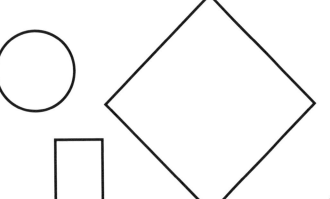
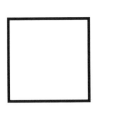
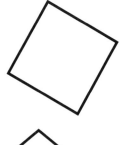
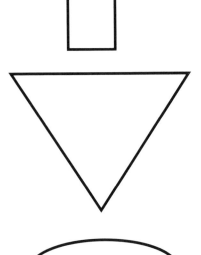

© Carson-Dellosa

PLACE
STICKER
HERE

Trace the dashed lines.

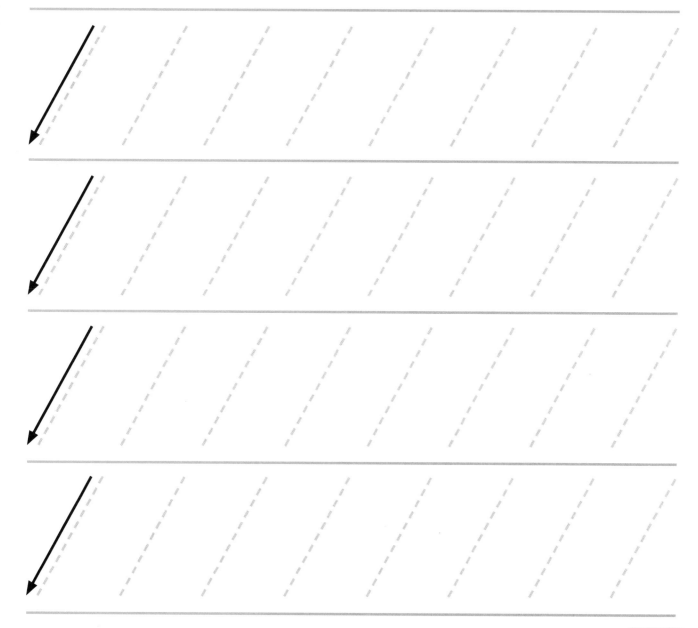

© Carson-Dellosa

DAY 3

This is a triangle.

Color the triangles.

© Carson-Dellosa

PLACE
STICKER
HERE

Trace the dashed lines.

© Carson-Dellosa

DAY 4

This is a circle.

Color the circles.

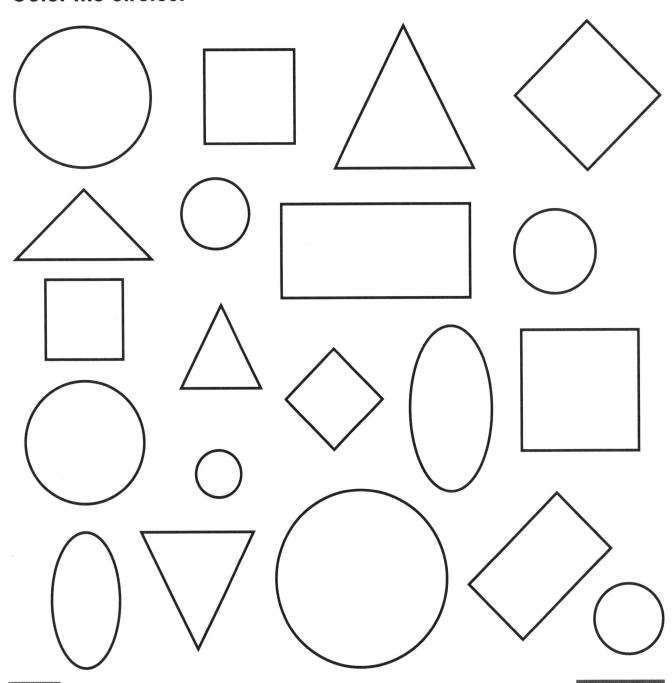

© Carson-Dellosa

PLACE STICKER HERE

Trace the dashed lines.

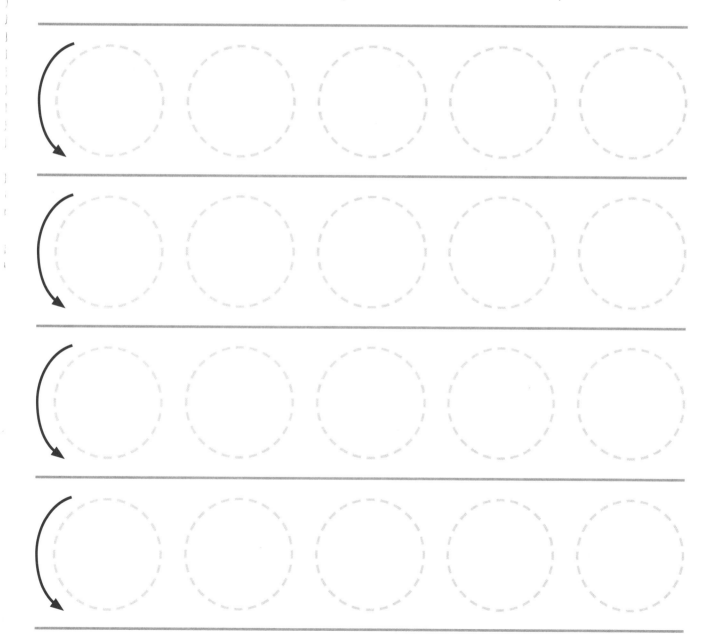

© Carson-Dellosa

DAY 5

This is a rectangle.

Color the rectangles.

© Carson-Dellosa

PLACE
STICKER
HERE

Trace the dashed lines.

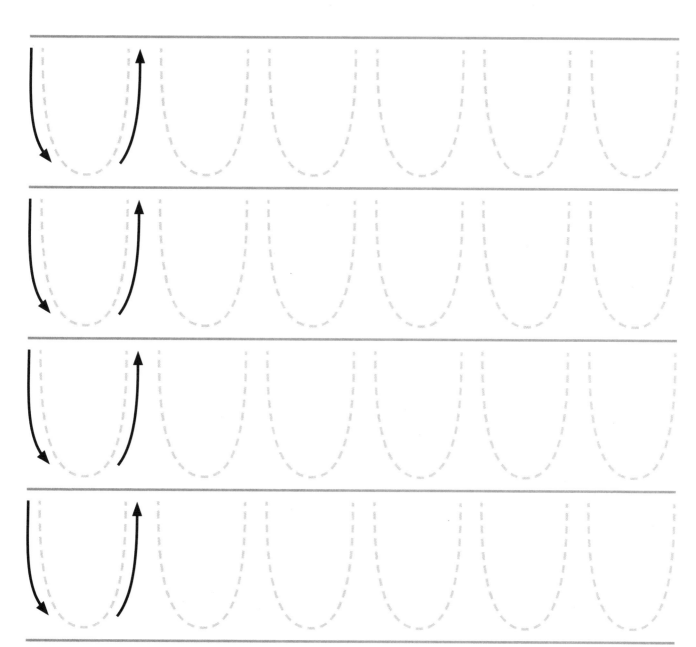

© Carson-Dellosa

DAY 6

This is an oval.

Color the ovals.

© Carson-Dellosa

PLACE
STICKER
HERE

Count 1 castle.

Color 1 crown.

© Carson-Dellosa

DAY 7

Use a different color of crayon to trace each kite string. Circle the child who is flying the green kite.

© Carson-Dellosa

PLACE STICKER HERE

Count 2 garages.

Color 2 cars.

© Carson-Dellosa

DAY 8

This is a rhombus.

Color the rhombuses.

© Carson-Dellosa

PLACE
STICKER
HERE

Count 3 pencils.

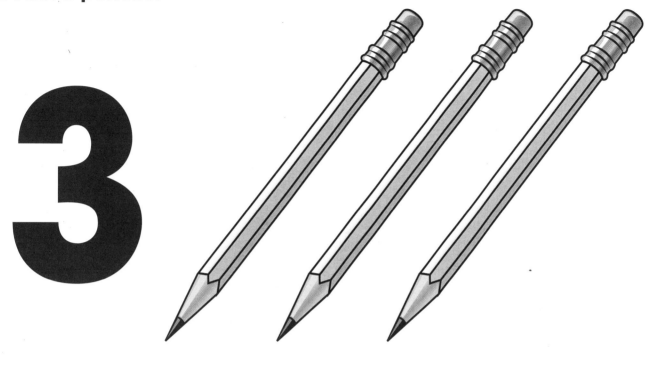

Color 3 books.

© Carson-Dellosa

DAY 9

Use the key to color each shape.

◇ = **red** □ = **blue** △ = **orange**
◻ = **green** ○ = **yellow** ⬭ = **purple**

© Carson-Dellosa

PLACE STICKER HERE

Count 4 guitars.

Color 4 bells.

© Carson-Dellosa

DAY 10

Draw an X on each object that is shaped like a circle.

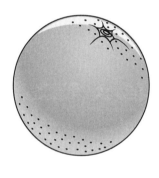

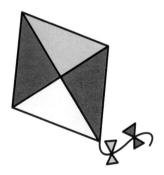

© Carson-Dellosa

PLACE
STICKER
HERE

Count 5 flowerpots.

Color 5 flowers.

© Carson-Dellosa

DAY 11

Count the objects in each row. Circle the number that tells how many.

	1 2 3 4 5
(five balls)	1 2 3 4 5
(three suns)	1 2 3 4 5
(one hat)	1 2 3 4 5
(two umbrellas)	1 2 3 4 5
(four pencils)	1 2 3 4 5

© Carson-Dellosa

PLACE STICKER HERE

Count 6 fishbowls.

Color 6 fish.

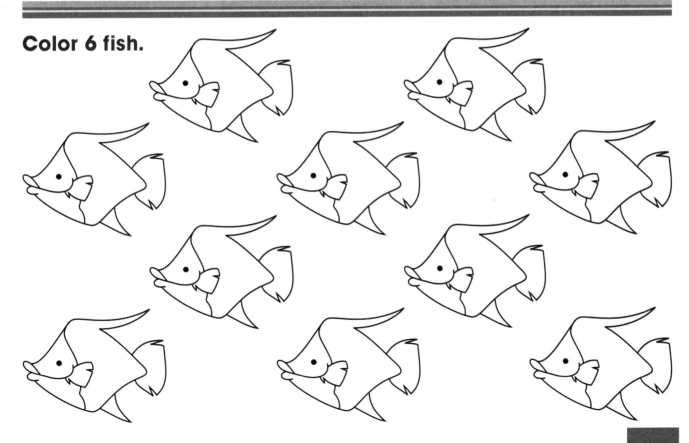

© Carson-Dellosa

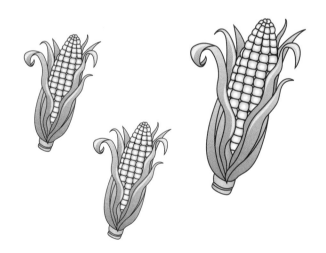

DAY 12

Circle the objects in each set that are the same size.

Example:

© Carson-Dellosa

PLACE STICKER HERE

Count 7 umbrellas.

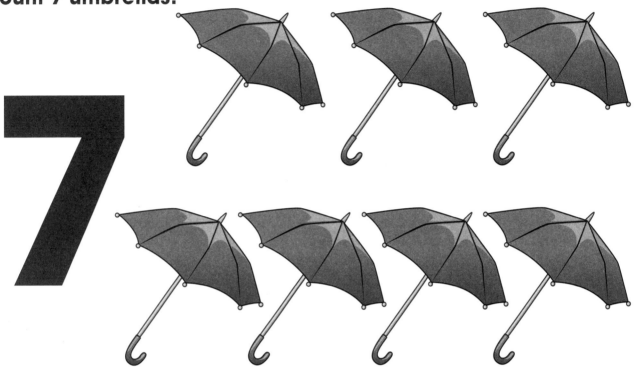

Color 7 clouds.

© Carson-Dellosa

DAY 13

Draw a line to match each big shape to the same little shape. Color the matching shapes the same color.

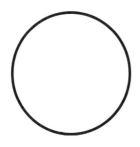

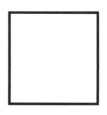

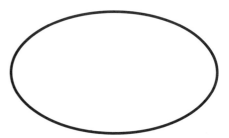

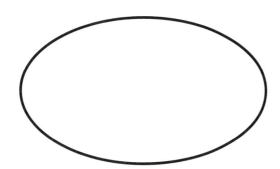
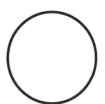

© Carson-Dellosa

PLACE
STICKER
HERE

Count 8 leaves.

Color 8 apples.

© Carson-Dellosa

DAY 14

Count the objects in each set. Write the number on the line.

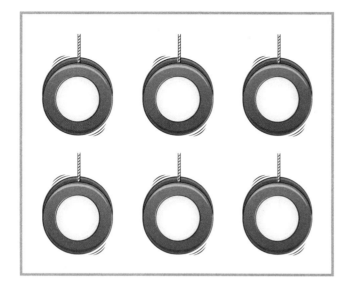

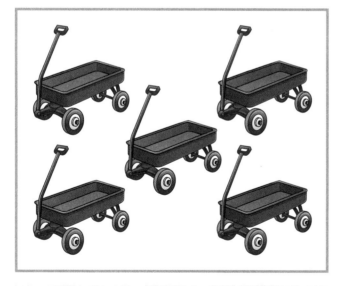

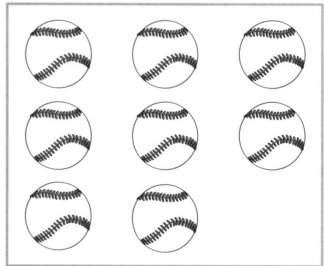

© Carson-Dellosa

PLACE STICKER HERE

Count 9 sandwiches.

Color 9 glasses of juice.

© Carson-Dellosa

DAY 15

Connect the dots from 0 to 5. Start at the ⭐. Color the picture.

© Carson-Dellosa

PLACE
STICKER
HERE

Count 10 paint cans.

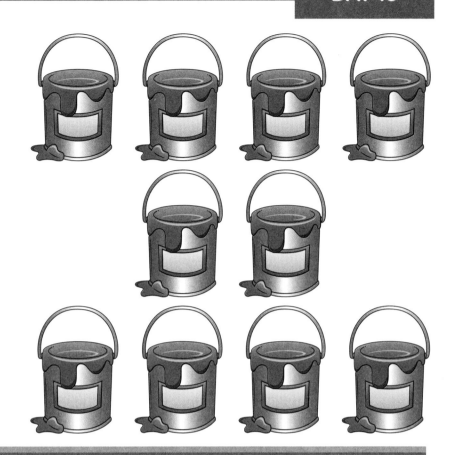

Color 10 paintbrushes.

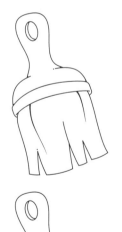   

© Carson-Dellosa

DAY 16

Connect the dots from 0 to 10. Start at the ★. Color the picture.

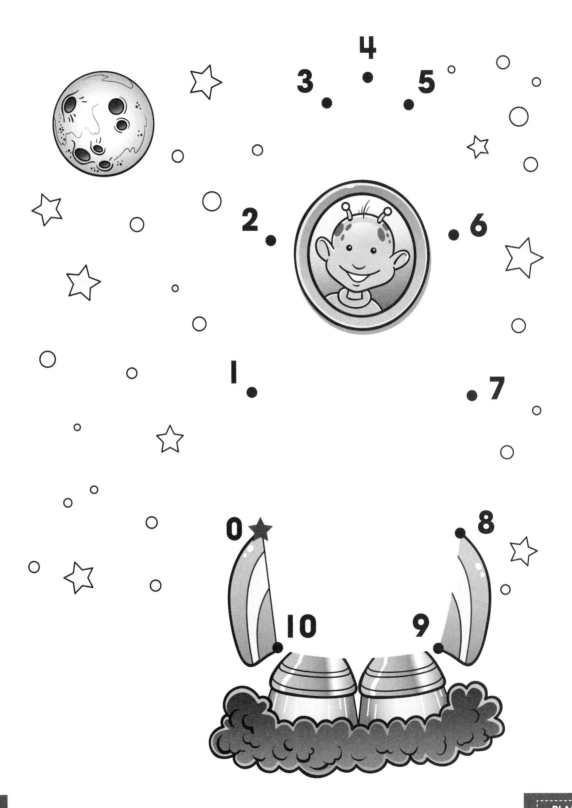

© Carson-Dellosa

PLACE STICKER HERE

Draw a line through the numbers 0 to 10 to help the horse find the hay.

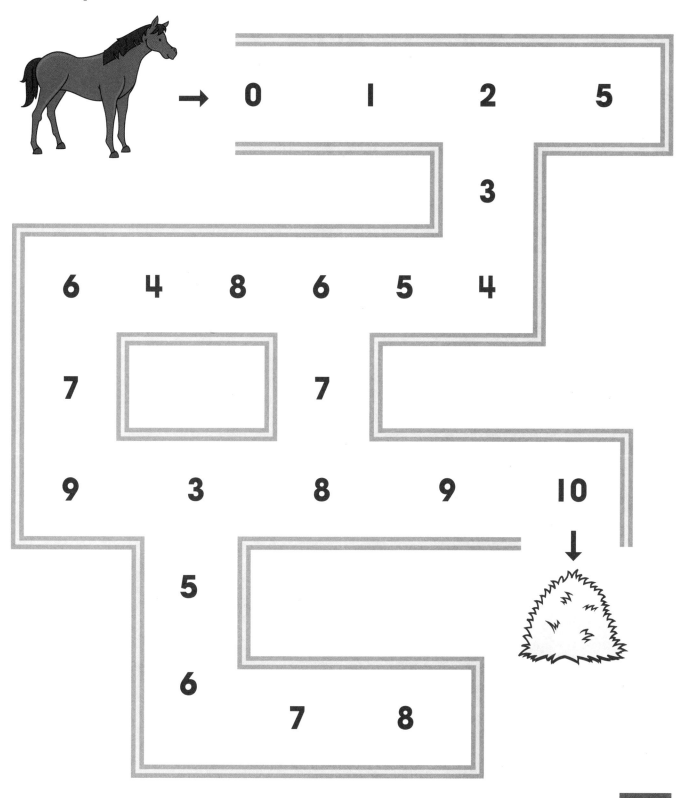

© Carson-Dellosa

DAY 17

Use the key to color each shape.

◇ = **red**   ▭ = **blue**   △ = **orange**
▢ = **green**   ○ = **yellow**   ◖ = **purple**

© Carson-Dellosa

PLACE
STICKER
HERE

Draw a line in each set to match a big object to a big object.
Draw a line in each set to match a little object to a little object.

Example:

DAY 18

Count the objects in each set. Circle the number that tells how many.

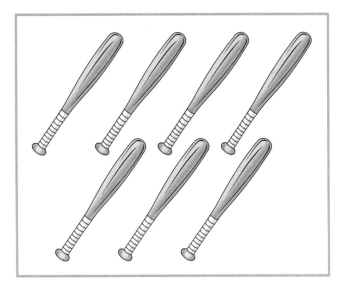

7   9   10

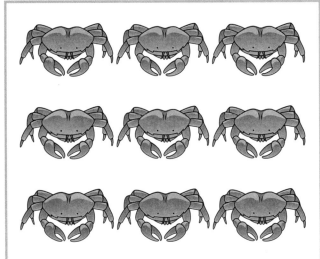

8   9   10

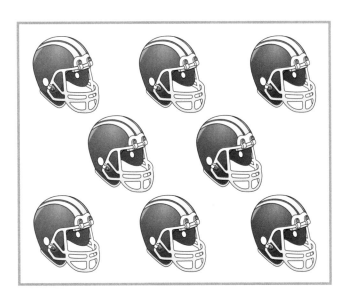

7   8   9

8   9   10

© Carson-Dellosa

PLACE STICKER HERE

Draw a line to help the dog find the bone.

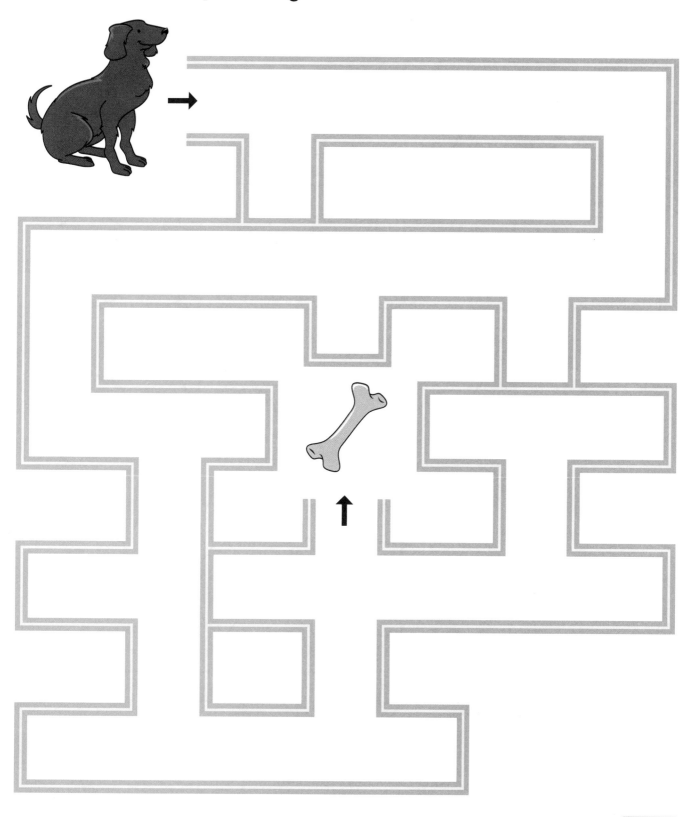

© Carson-Dellosa

DAY 19

Color the first shape in each row. Color the matching shapes the same color.

© Carson-Dellosa

PLACE
STICKER
HERE

Trace each shape with a different color of crayon.

© Carson-Dellosa

DAY 20

Draw a line to match each shape to an object with almost the same shape.

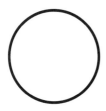

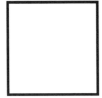

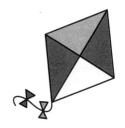

YIELD

© Carson-Dellosa

PLACE STICKER HERE

Freezing Water

What happens to water when it is placed in a freezer? What happens when it is taken out of a freezer?

Materials:
- eyedropper
- ice cube tray
- water

Procedure:
Help your child use the eyedropper to place 3–5 drops of water into each section of the ice cube tray. Put the ice cube tray in the freezer for approximately 10 minutes or until the water is frozen. When frozen, remove a piece of ice from the ice cube tray and place it in your child's hand. Ask your child the questions below.

1. What happened to the water in the freezer? _____

   _____

2. What happened to the ice when you held it? _____

   _____

3. Did it take longer to freeze the water or to melt the ice? _____

   _____

4. Why do you think the water froze? _____

   _____

5. Why do you think the ice melted? _____

   _____

© Carson-Dellosa

Stretch and Guess

Ask your child to think of three animals. How does she think these animals stretch when they wake up?

Have her practice stretching like the animals she chose. For example, if she chose a cat, she might sit on her knees and place her palms flat on the floor. Then, she could arch her back like a cat. She can even meow if she wants!

Once she has practiced her animal stretches, ask her to show them to a family audience. Can your family members guess the animals she chose?

Number "Show-How"

Let your child show how well he knows numbers! Begin by saying a number. Have your child try to bend and stretch into that number's shape. For number one, he might stand on his toes and straighten his arms overhead.

To demonstrate more difficult numbers, such as two, he will have to be creative and flexible. He may curve his arms and kneel on the floor. In some cases, he may have to give a verbal description as well.

Later, allow him to show off his number "show-how" to a family audience and ask them to guess or even match his stretchy numbers.

Taking Turns

Help your child make a book about taking turns. Fold 3–4 sheets of blank paper in half and staple the sheets along the fold. Title the book *I Take Turns!* and allow your child to decorate the cover.

Ask your child to draw pictures of how she takes turns during a day or week. For example, your child could draw a picture of herself waiting for a turn to drink from a water fountain. Once your child has filled the pages of her book, invite her to share her pictures and explain how each one shows that she is taking turns.

The Three Rs of Respect

Discuss with your child what it means to respect something using examples to which he can relate. Explain how important it is for your child to be considerate of another person's feelings, possessions, and ideas.

Introduce the three Rs of respect: respect for oneself, respect for others, and respect for the earth. Talk about how he can show respect for each. Then, help him make a list of actions he can take this summer to show his respect for the above. Post the list in a visible location to serve as a convenient respect reminder.

Respect Myself—I can eat healthy food.

I can exercise with Mom.

Respect Others—I can knock on the door to Thad's room.

I can feed Charlie his doggie dinner on time.

Respect Earth—I can turn off the water while I'm brushing my teeth.

I can recycle paper, cans, and plastic bottles.

© Carson-Dellosa

Take It Outside!

Play "I See Shapes" outside. Find a comfortable place to sit with your child. In this game, the first player must find something that is a distinct shape and start the game by naming the shape. For example, you might see a trampoline and say, "I see a circle." Then, describe the object in a variety of ways, such as by color and size. Play until you have tested your child's knowledge of several shapes. Then, allow him to find and name different shapes and describe the objects to you.

Grab your gardening gloves and play in the dirt! Find a sandy or dusty area. Invite your child to use her finger to practice drawing shapes, numbers, and letters in the sand or dirt. Join your child by drawing your own shapes, letters, and numbers. Then, quiz her knowledge of these key concepts. Make it fun and interactive by drawing two different shapes, letters, or numbers. Name one shape for her to identify. After she identifies the correct shape, allow her to erase the incorrect shape.

Go on a number hike! As you hike, challenge your child to count groups of things. How many ladybugs are on that leaf? How many cars are parked on the block? Look for opportunities throughout the summer to help your child notice numbers. Whether it is the prices on a menu or the distance on a highway sign, show your child how important numbers are in his growing world.

* See page ii.

© Carson-Dellosa

Monthly Goals

Think of three goals that you would like to set for yourself this month. For example, you may want to spend extra time reading with your family. Have an adult help you write your goals on the lines.

Place a sticker next to each goal you complete. Feel proud that you have met your goals!

1. _____ PLACE STICKER HERE

2. _____ PLACE STICKER HERE

3. _____ PLACE STICKER HERE

Word List

The following words are used in this section. They are good words for you to know. Read each word aloud with an adult. When you see a word from this list on a page, circle it with your favorite color of crayon.

black	orange
blue	purple
brown	red
green	set
many	yellow

© Carson-Dellosa

Introduction to Strength

At the end of this section are fitness and character development activities that focus on strength. These activities are designed to get your child moving and thinking about strengthening his body and his character. Complete these activities throughout the month as time allows.

Physical Strength

Like flexibility, strength is necessary for a child to be healthy. Many children think that strong people are people who can lift an enormous amount of weight. However, strength is more than the ability to pick up heavy barbells. Explain that strength is built over time and point out to your child how much stronger he has become since he was a toddler. At that time, he could pedal his tricycle down the sidewalk. Now, he can run across a baseball field.

Everyday activities and many fun exercises provide opportunities for children to gain strength. Your child can carry grocery bags to build muscle in his arms and ride a bicycle to develop strength in his legs. Classic exercises such as push-ups and chin-ups are also fantastic strength builders.

Help your child set realistic, achievable goals to improve his physical strength based on the activities that he enjoys. Over the summer months, offer encouragement and praise as your child becomes stronger and accomplishes his strength goals.

Strength of Character

As your child is building his physical strength, guide him to work on his inner strength as well. Explain that having strong character means standing up for his values, even if others do not agree with his viewpoint. Tell him it is not always easy to show inner strength. Discuss real-life examples, such as a time that he was teased by another child at the playground. How did he use his inner strength to handle this situation?

Remind your child that inner strength can be shown in many ways. For example, your child can show strength by being honest, standing up for someone who needs help, and putting his best efforts into every task. Use your time together over the summer to help your child develop a strong sense of self, both physically and emotionally. Look for moments to acknowledge when he has demonstrated strength of character so that he can see his positive growth on the inside as well as on the outside.

© Carson-Dellosa

Count 11 baseballs.

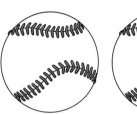   

Color 11 caps.

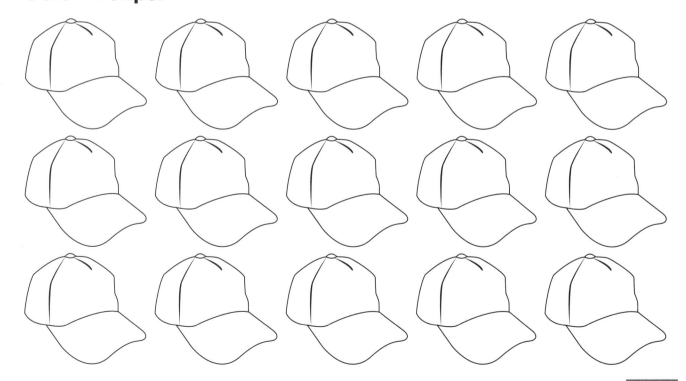

© Carson-Dellosa

DAY 1

Count the objects in each set. Circle the number that tells how many.

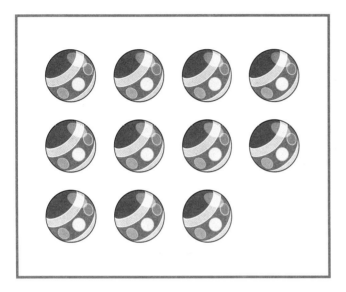

IO   II

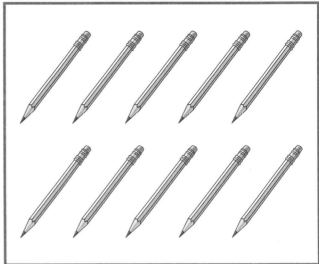

IO   II

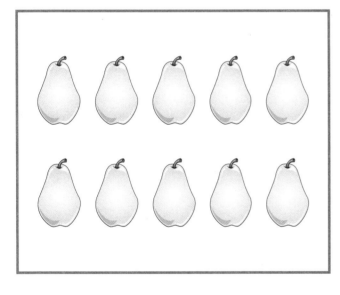

IO   II

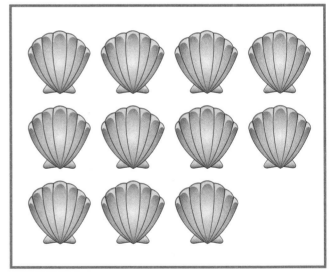

IO   II

© Carson-Dellosa

PLACE
STICKER
HERE

Count 12 moons.

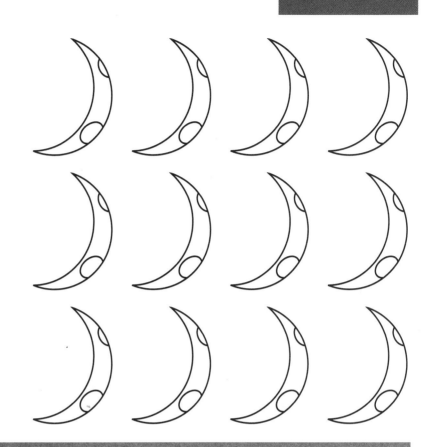

Color 12 stars.

© Carson-Dellosa

DAY 2

Color the pictures red.

strawberry

stop sign

cherries

apple

© Carson-Dellosa

PLACE
STICKER
HERE

  apple

Trace and write each letter.

Circle the pictures that begin like .

dog

rainbow

astronaut

alligator

ant

© Carson-Dellosa

DAY 3

Color the pictures orange.

pumpkin

carrot

fish

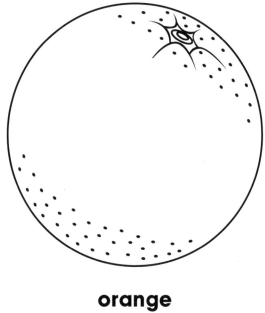

orange

© Carson-Dellosa

PLACE
STICKER
HERE

Bb

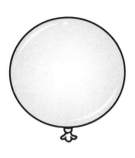

balloon

Trace and write each letter.

B B -

b b -

Circle the pictures that begin like .

bird

ball

sock

bee

horse

DAY 4

Color the pictures yellow.

sun

chick

lemon

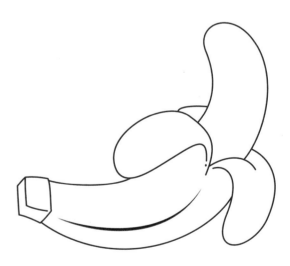

banana

© Carson-Dellosa

PLACE
STICKER
HERE

  cake

Trace and write each letter.

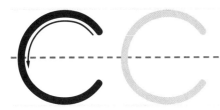

Circle the pictures that begin like .

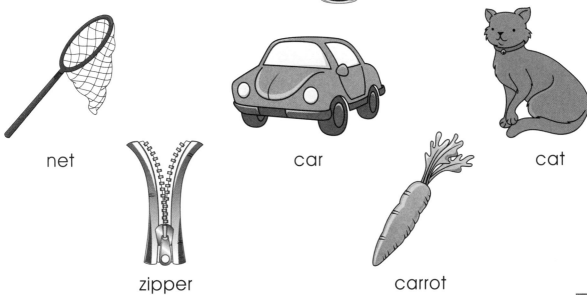

net

zipper

car

carrot

cat

© Carson-Dellosa

DAY 5

Color the pictures green.

tree

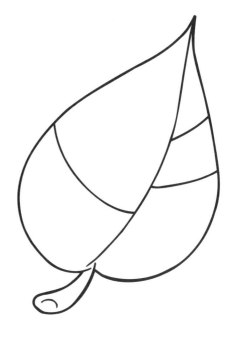

leaf

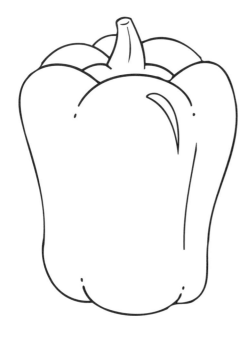

pepper

frog

© Carson-Dellosa

PLACE
STICKER
HERE

Dd

dog

Trace and write each letter.

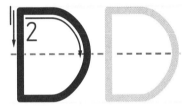

- -

- -

Circle the pictures that begin like .

desk

fish

jar

doll

duck

© Carson-Dellosa

DAY 6

Color the pictures blue.

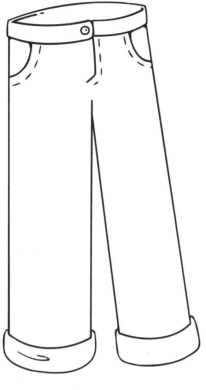

jeans

bluebird

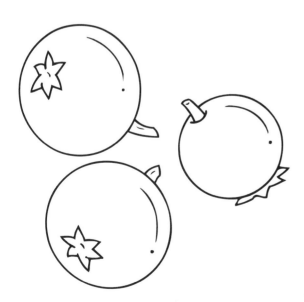

blueberries

ribbon

© Carson-Dellosa

PLACE STICKER HERE

E e

 *egg*

Trace and write each letter.

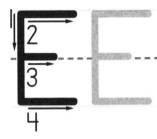

Circle the pictures that begin like ⬭ **.**

eggplant

violin

envelope

banana

elephant

© Carson-Dellosa

DAY 7

Color the pictures purple.

grapes

pansy

plum

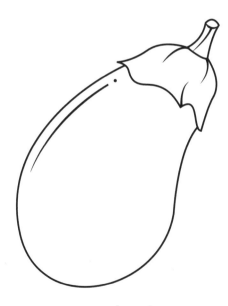

eggplant

© Carson-Dellosa

PLACE STICKER HERE

fish

Trace and write each letter.

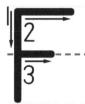 F -

 f -

Circle the pictures that begin like .

foot

fan

ball

feather

sun

© Carson-Dellosa

DAY 8

Color the pictures black.

tire

bear

top hat

crow

© Carson-Dellosa

PLACE STICKER HERE

G g

guitar

Trace and write each letter.

g

Circle the pictures that begin like .

gift

turtle

can

goggles

goat

© Carson-Dellosa

DAY 9

Color the pictures brown.

teddy bear

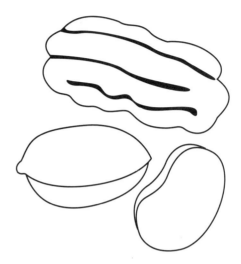

nuts

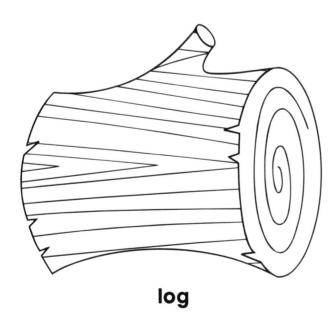

log

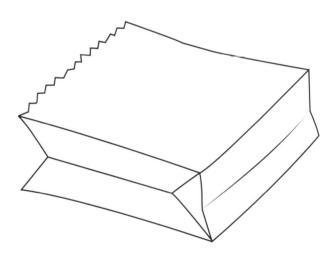

paper bag

© Carson-Dellosa

PLACE
STICKER
HERE

  horse

Trace and write each letter.

- -

- -

Circle the pictures that begin like .

hammer

 hat

 house

apple

fork

© Carson-Dellosa

DAY 10

Count the objects in each set. Circle the number that tells how many.

3   4   5

3   4   5

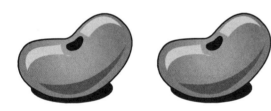

2   3   4

4   5   6

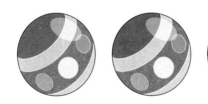

3   4   5

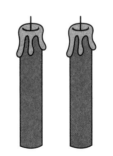 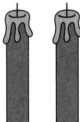 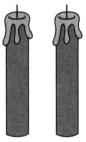

5   6   7

© Carson-Dellosa

PLACE STICKER HERE

igloo

Trace and write each letter.

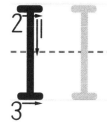

Circle the pictures that begin like .

iguana

duck

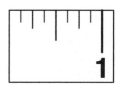

inch

lock

ink

© Carson-Dellosa

DAY 11

Count the objects in each set. Circle the number that tells how many.

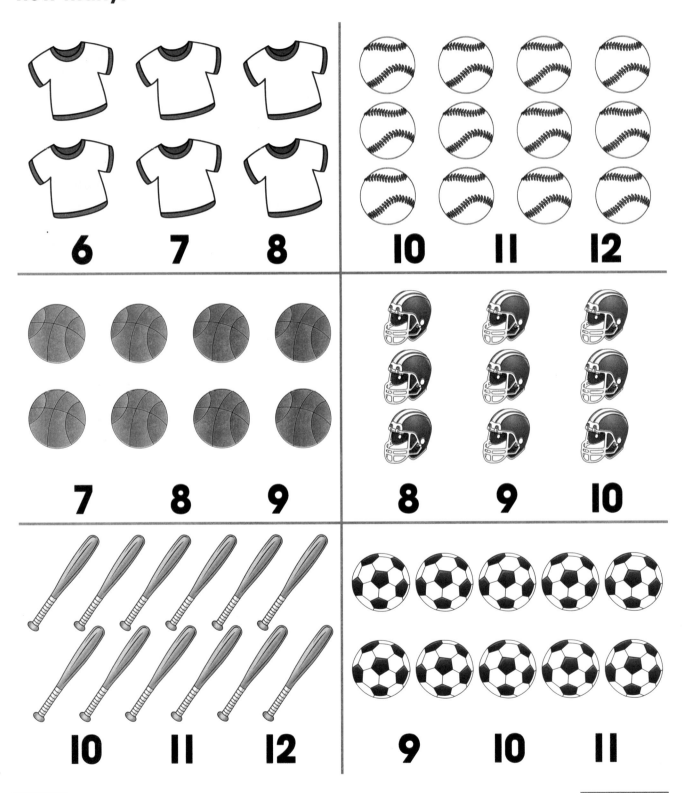

6   7   8   10   11   12

7   8   9   8   9   10

10   11   12   9   10   11

© Carson-Dellosa

PLACE STICKER HERE

  jar

Trace and write each letter.

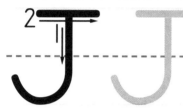

Circle the pictures that begin like .

jack-in-the-box   jet   goat

 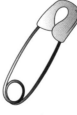

jelly beans   pin

71

DAY 12

Color each picture.

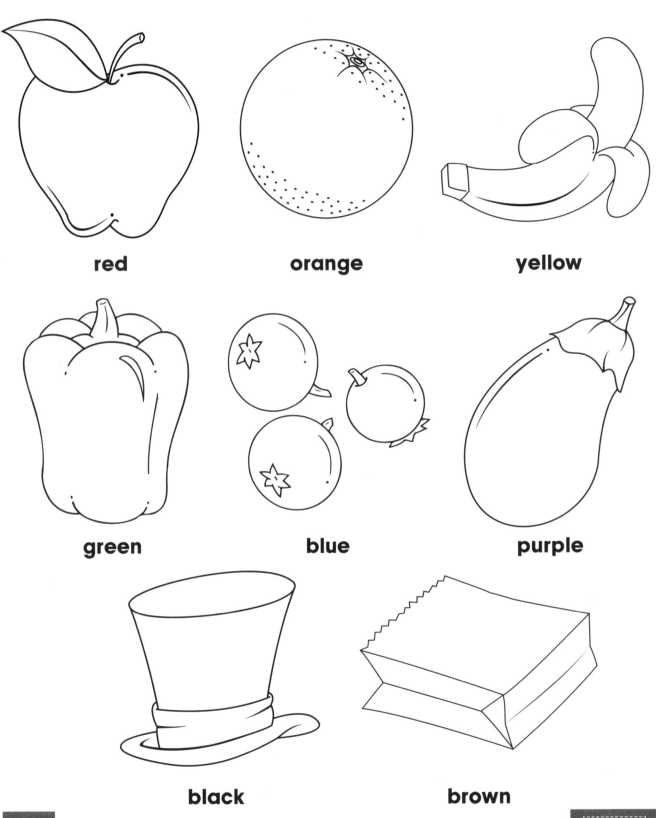

red   orange   yellow

green   blue   purple

black   brown

© Carson-Dellosa

PLACE
STICKER
HERE

Kk

king

Trace and write each letter.

Circle the pictures that begin like .

keys

kite

pencil

kangaroo

tiger

© Carson-Dellosa

DAY 13

Say the name of each picture. Circle the letter that matches the beginning sound.

Example:

a   (b)   l

f   j   d

f   d   i

c   e   b

j   c   h

g   a   k

m   i   c

d   k   j

g   h   l

© Carson-Dellosa

PLACE STICKER HERE

  lemon

Trace and write each letter.

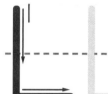

Circle the pictures that begin like .

lamp

hammer

book

lion

leaf

© Carson-Dellosa

DAY 14

Count and color the correct number of objects in each row.

Color 3 purple.

Color 4 orange.

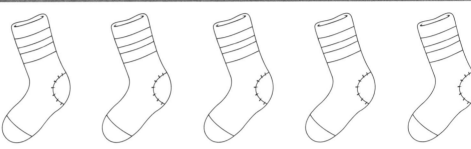

Color 2 yellow.

Color 5 red.

Color 1 green.

 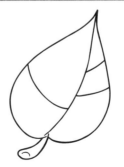 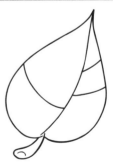

© Carson-Dellosa

PLACE STICKER HERE

  moon

Trace and write each letter.

Circle the pictures that begin like .

mop

kite

tree

mitten

mouse

© Carson-Dellosa

DAY 15

Count the shapes in each set. Circle the number that tells how many.

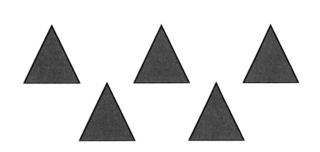

5   6   7 | 2   3

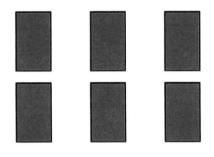

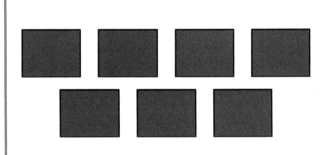

5   6   7   7   8   9

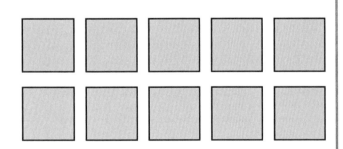

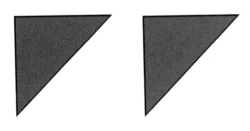

8   9   10   2   3   4

© Carson-Dellosa

PLACE
STICKER
HERE

Nn

nail

Trace and write each letter.

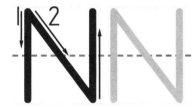

Circle the pictures that begin like .

nuts

lemon

net

carrot

nest

© Carson-Dellosa

Continue each pattern.

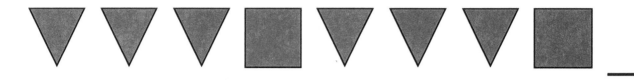

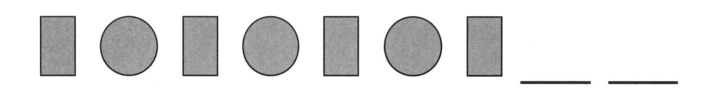

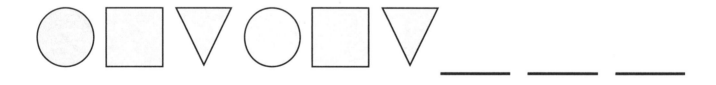

© Carson-Dellosa

PLACE STICKER HERE

  ostrich

Trace and write each letter.

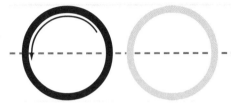

Circle the pictures that begin like .

bone

olive

octagon

octopus

wagon

© Carson-Dellosa

DAY 17

Use the key to color each shape.

◇ = **red**   □ = **purple**   ◁ = **orange**
▱ = **blue**   ○ = **yellow**   ◯ = **green**

© Carson-Dellosa

PLACE
STICKER
HERE

P p  pumpkin

Trace and write each letter.

___

Circle the pictures that begin like .

yarn

igloo

pear

penguin

pie

© Carson-Dellosa

DAY 18

Circle the living things.

bird   doll   flower

TV   fish   turtle

dog   car

© Carson-Dellosa

PLACE
STICKER
HERE

queen

Trace and write each letter.

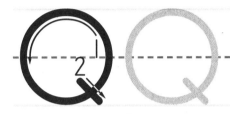

Circle the pictures that begin like .

yo-yo

quilt

quarter

ant

quail

© Carson-Dellosa

DAY 19

Draw a line to match each card to the envelope with the same shape and size.

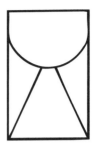

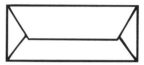

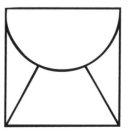

© Carson-Dellosa

PLACE STICKER HERE

Rr

rocket

Trace and write each letter.

Circle the pictures that begin like .

rock

rabbit

giraffe

ring

moon

© Carson-Dellosa

DAY 20

Circle the uppercase letters in each set that are the same.

Example:

(F) E (F)
B (F) A

P R R
R H D

W W V
W Y W

G O G
G Y C

E D X
D D L

H H H
Y H Z

O Q G
Q Q C

N M N
N N Z

L F T
C T T

© Carson-Dellosa

PLACE STICKER HERE

Absorbing Water

Which substances absorb the most water?

Materials:
- eyedropper
- scissors
- cup of water
- cardboard egg carton
- spoon

Substances:
- paper towel
- sponge
- toilet paper
- dirt
- aluminum foil
- newspaper
- waxed paper
- cotton ball
- cloth
- sand
- construction paper

Procedure: Help your child place a small amount of each substance into a separate section of the egg carton. Use the spoon to place the dirt and sand into the egg carton. Use the eyedropper to slowly add 5–10 drops of water to each section. Add the same amount of water to each substance. Observe whether the substance absorbed or did not absorb the water. Ask your child the questions below.

1. Which substances absorbed water? _____

_____

2. Which substances did not absorb water? _____

_____

3. Which substance absorbed the most water? _____

4. Which substances could you use to clean up spilled milk? _____

_____

© Carson-Dellosa

Push-Up Pick-Me-Up

Show your child how to do a push-up. Talk about how much upper body strength a push-up takes and let her try to complete one. If she is successful, have her attempt to do another. If she has trouble completing one push-up, celebrate her effort and talk about how difficult this exercise can be (especially if you had trouble doing it). Then, help her complete a modified push-up with her bent knees and her feet on the ground. After she has completed a few push-ups successfully, challenge her to complete as many push-ups as she can. Remind her to keep her back straight. Encourage her to continue doing sets of push-ups several times a week. At the end of the summer, see how many sets your child can complete. Discuss any demonstrated improvements with your child.

Wall Sits

Have your child stand straight against a wall. Ask him to bring his legs out in front of him. Next, he should bend his knees and slide down the wall until he is in a sitting position. Now, have him stand up and "sit" as many times as he can. Let him practice this every day for one week. Write how many wall sits he completes next to each day below. What does your child notice as his legs get stronger?

Sunday _____   Monday _____

Tuesday _____   Wednesday _____

Thursday _____   Friday _____

Saturday _____

© Carson-Dellosa

"Tug-of-Peace"

Get your family or neighbors involved in a friendly game of tug-of-war. Use a strong rope, or tie several sturdy pieces of fabric together. Mark the midpoint with a brightly colored scarf and place a straight marker, such as a ruler, on the ground.

For the first round, assign unequal teams by placing the strongest players, or more players, on one team. After the team with the unfair advantage wins, ask your child to tell you why she thinks that team won. Then, discuss what it means to be fair using examples to which she can relate, such as treating others the way she wants to be treated.

Then, help your child reassign teams so that the game is played more fairly. Celebrate as a group by having a summer snack, such as watermelon, cut into fair, equal portions!

Invitation to Integrity

Discuss with your child what it means to have integrity using examples to which he can relate, such as standing up for what he believes in. Then, appoint a time to hold a family meeting to talk about your family's values. This meeting should include a discussion about the standards and rules your family lives by or will agree to live by.

Next, provide your child with craft materials and have him create an invitation to the family meeting for each family member. Make sure he includes the time, date, and place to meet. Have him deliver the invitations or present them during a family time, such as breakfast or dinner.

Involve your child as much as possible during the meeting. Use poster board and a marker to list your family's key beliefs in simple language. After the meeting, post the list in visible location as a positive reminder of what integrity means to your family.

* See page ii.

© Carson-Dellosa

Take It Outside!

Clean up your neighborhood with your child. Put on protective clothing and gloves and get two heavy-duty trash bags so that you and your child can pick up litter outside your home, at a park, or along the beach. As you are practicing the character trait of respect for the earth, use this time to talk about the importance of taking care of the world around you. Listen to your child's ideas and let him brainstorm possibilities for making the earth a better place to live.

Make a fun outdoor treasure hunt with an alphabet twist. Have your child write the letters of the alphabet along the left side of a sheet of paper. Invite her to take her letter list and a pencil outside to search for outdoor objects that begin with each letter of the alphabet. For challenging letters, such as *q* and *x*, be more flexible by helping her to record a *quiet butterfly* or an *extra flower*.

Summer is the perfect time to start a collection. Whether your child is interested in rocks, leaves, or another item found in nature, encourage him to collect a variety of the objects. Provide him with a container to gather his treasures. Once he has found several items, have him organize them into groups based on similarities. For example, he could group the objects by color, shape, or size. When his collection is complete, help him find a way to decorate and display his objects.

* See page ii.

© Carson-Dellosa

Monthly Goals

Think of three goals that you would like to set for yourself this month. For example, you may want to learn three new words each week. Have an adult help you write your goals on the lines.

Place a sticker next to each goal you complete. Feel proud that you have met your goals!

1. _____

2. _____
PLACE STICKER HERE

3. _____
PLACE STICKER HERE

Word List

The following words are used in this section. They are good words for you to know. Read each word aloud with an adult. When you see a word from this list on a page, circle it with your favorite color of crayon.

box	more
count	name
find	number
letter	sound
line	word

© Carson-Dellosa

Introduction to Endurance

At the end of this section are fitness and character development activities that focus on endurance. These activities are designed to get your child moving and thinking about developing her physical and mental stamina. Complete these activities throughout the month as time allows.

Physical Endurance

Many children seem to have endless energy and can run, jump, and play for hours. But, other children have not yet developed that kind of endurance. Improving endurance requires regular aerobic exercise, which causes the heart to beat faster and the person to breathe harder. As a result of regular aerobic activity, the heart grows stronger and the blood cells deliver oxygen to the body more efficiently. There are many ways for a child to get an aerobic workout that does not feel like exercise. Jumping rope and playing tag are examples.

Summer provides a variety of opportunities to bolster your child's endurance. If you see your child head for the TV, suggest an activity that will get her moving instead. Explain that while there are times when a relaxing activity is valuable, it is important to take advantage of the warm mornings and sunny days to go outdoors. Leave the less active times for when it is dark, too hot, or raining. Explain the importance of physical activity and invite her to join you for a walk, a bicycle ride, or a game of basketball.

Endurance and Character Development

Endurance applies to the mind as well as to the body. Explain to your child that *endurance* means to stick with something. Children can demonstrate mental endurance every day. For example, staying with a task when she might want to quit and keeping at it until it is complete are ways that a child can show endurance.

Take advantage of summertime to help your child practice her mental endurance. Look for situations where she might seem frustrated or bored. Perhaps she asked to take swimming lessons, but after a few early morning classes, she is not having as much fun as she imagined. Turn this dilemma into a learning tool. It is important that children feel some ownership in decision making, so guide her to some key points to consider, such as how she asked to take lessons. Remind her that she has taken only a few lessons, so she might become more used to the early morning lessons. Let her know that she has options to make the experience more enjoyable, such as going to bed earlier or sleeping a few extra minutes during the morning car ride. Explain that quitting should be the last resort. Teaching your child to endure will help her as she continues to develop into a happy, healthy person.

© Carson-Dellosa

S s

sun

Trace and write each letter.

Circle the pictures that begin like .

sandwich

keys

socks

pear

soap

© Carson-Dellosa

DAY I

Circle the things that are not living.

butterfly

balloon

mug

penguin

book

house

van

caterpillar

gift

© Carson-Dellosa

PLACE STICKER HERE

turtle

Trace and write each letter.

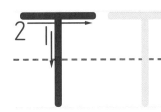

Circle the pictures that begin like .

teddy bear

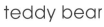

net

tent

hand

turkey

© Carson-Dellosa

DAY 2

Circle the lowercase letters in each set that are the same.

Example:

(e) f i	p d o	c s o
(e) (e) p	d n d	s s s
r n r	v v y	p d d
r b i	v d v	d b d
g p g	i j i	j g p
y g g	i n i	j j y

© Carson-Dellosa

PLACE
STICKER
HERE

U u

umbrella

Trace and write each letter.

Circle the pictures that begin like .

undershirt

pumpkin

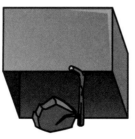

under

up

egg

© Carson-Dellosa

DAY 3

Circle the letter in each set that is different.

Example:

f (t) f f f f f   w v v v v v

L L L L L L Z   M N M M M M M

c c c c c e c   o o o o e o o

M W M M M M M   x v x x x x x

Q Q Q O Q Q Q   n n u n n n

G G G C G G G   o o a o o o o

© Carson-Dellosa

PLACE
STICKER
HERE

V v

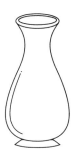

vase

Trace and write each letter.

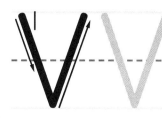

Circle the pictures that begin like .

van

vacuum

vest

yo-yo

banana

© Carson-Dellosa

DAY 4

Say the name of each picture. Circle the letter that matches the beginning sound.

Example:

r （s） t

n y t

q m p

w o k

u z r

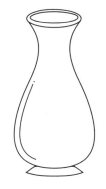

t v n

t n v

s q x

f l m

© Carson-Dellosa

PLACE STICKER HERE

  window

Trace and write each letter.

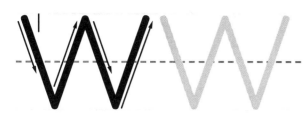

Circle the pictures that begin like .

mailbox

wagon

web

watch

jar

© Carson-Dellosa

DAY 5

Say the name of each picture. Circle the letter that matches the beginning sound.

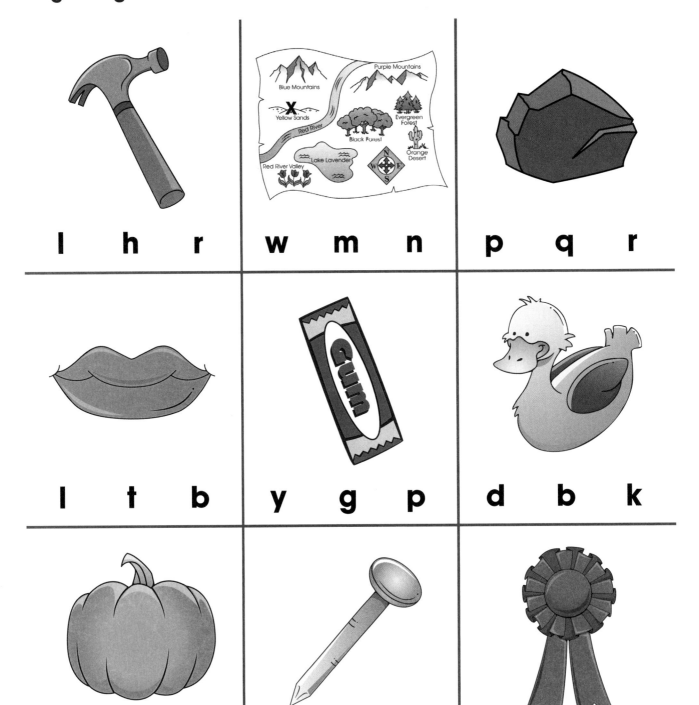

l   h   r   w   m   n   p   q   r

l   t   b   y   g   p   d   b   k

d   j   p   n   r   t   s   n   r

© Carson-Dellosa

PLACE STICKER HERE

X-ray

Trace and write each letter.

Circle the pictures that have the letter *x*, like .

box

queen

fox

ox

barn

© Carson-Dellosa

DAY 6

Count each kind of animal. Color one box for each animal you count.

© Carson-Dellosa

PLACE
STICKER
HERE

Y y  yak

Trace and write each letter.

Circle the pictures that begin like **.**

yogurt

yo-yo

lemon

rabbit

yarn

© Carson-Dellosa

DAY 7

Draw the correct number of shapes in each set.

Example:

2 squares	**4 circles**	**3 rectangles**
1 circle	**2 triangles**	**5 ovals**

© Carson-Dellosa

PLACE STICKER HERE

Z z

zigzag

Trace and write each letter.

Z Z — — — — — — — — — — — — — — — — — —

z z — — — — — — — — — — — — — — — — — —

Circle the pictures that begin like  .

zipper

guitar

zebra

zero

seal

© Carson-Dellosa

DAY 8

Draw a line through the numbers 1 to 12 to help the rocket find the moon.

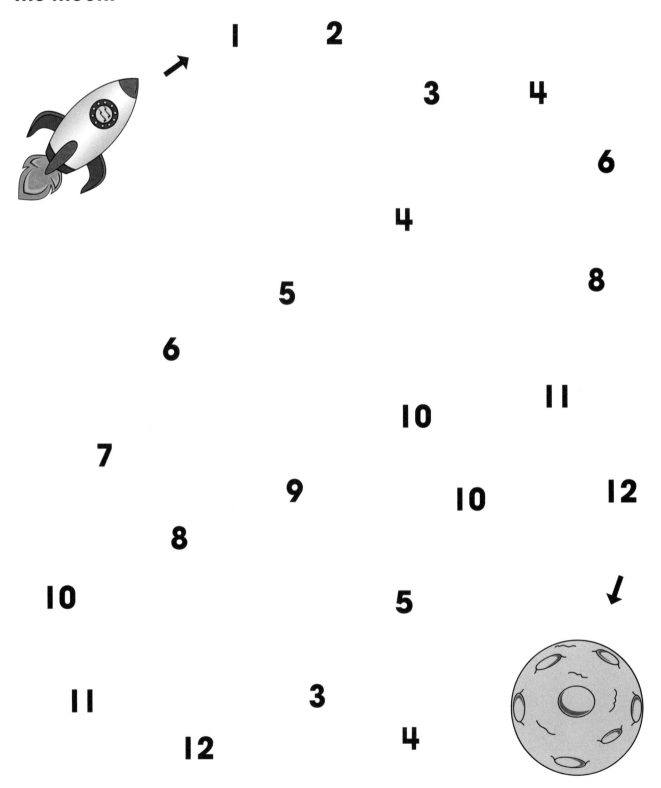

1   2

3   4

6

4

8

5

6

10

11

7

9

10   12

8

10   5

11   3

12   4

© Carson-Dellosa

PLACE
STICKER
HERE

Write the uppercase letters of the alphabet in order on the train cars. Circle each train car that has a letter from your first name.

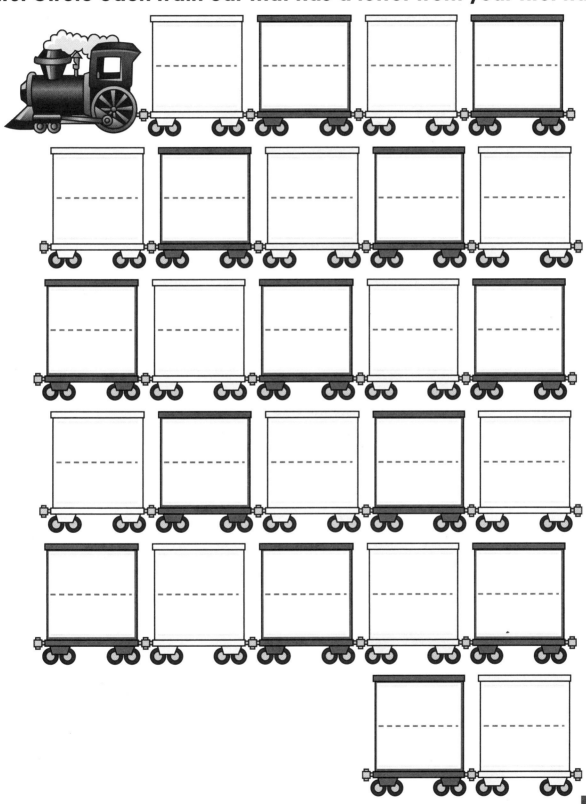

© Carson-Dellosa

DAY 9

Connect the dots from A to Z. Start at the ⭐. Color the picture.

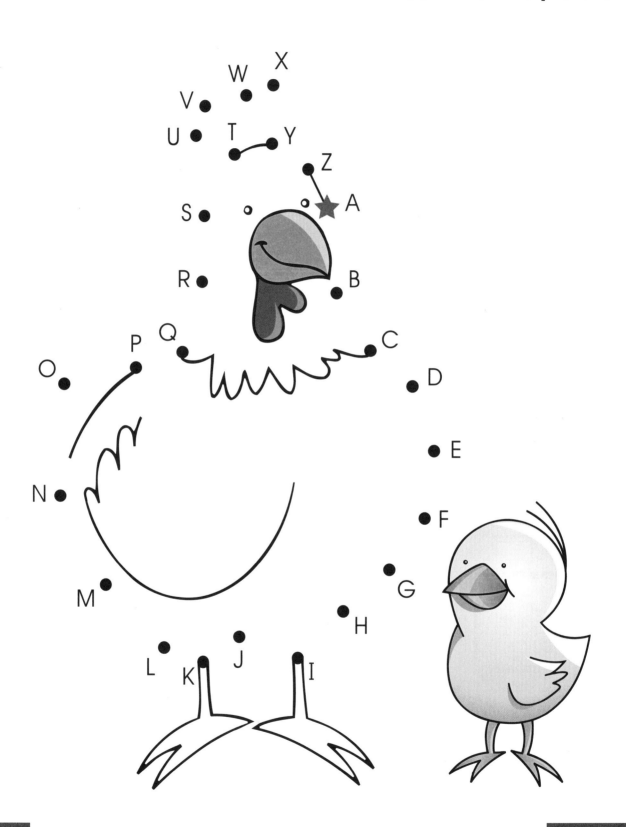

© Carson-Dellosa

PLACE STICKER HERE

Color each picture. Circle the correct color word.

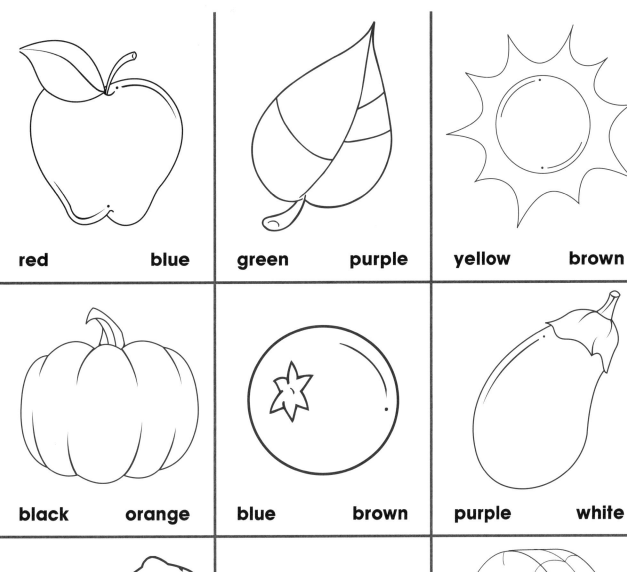

red blue	green purple	yellow brown
black orange	blue brown	purple white

 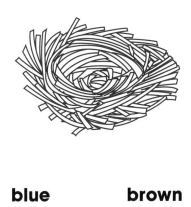 

white green	blue brown	orange black

© Carson-Dellosa

DAY 10

Draw a circle around each object you would find inside. Draw an X on each object you would find outside.

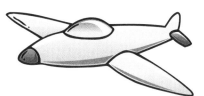

© Carson-Dellosa

PLACE STICKER HERE

Circle the things you can see.

flowers

teddy bear

music

car

rainbow

Circle the things you can hear.

laughter

doorbell

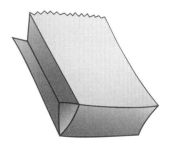

bag

pear

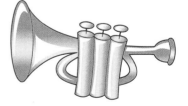

horn

© Carson-Dellosa

DAY 11

Circle the things you can taste.

| ice-cream cone | sandwich | house | apple |

Circle the things you can smell.

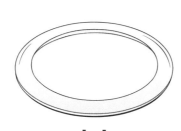

| orange | plate | flower | bread |

Circle the things you can touch.

| cat | teddy bear | hat | moon |

© Carson-Dellosa

PLACE STICKER HERE

Number the seasons from 1 to 4. Start with summer.

© Carson-Dellosa

DAY 12

Number the pictures in the order that they happened.

© Carson-Dellosa

PLACE STICKER HERE

Circle the object in each set that has more.

© Carson-Dellosa

Draw a line to match each animal to its home.

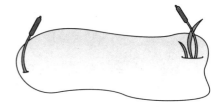

© Carson-Dellosa

PLACE
STICKER
HERE

Say the name of each picture. Draw a line from each little picture to the big picture that begins with the same sound.

Example:

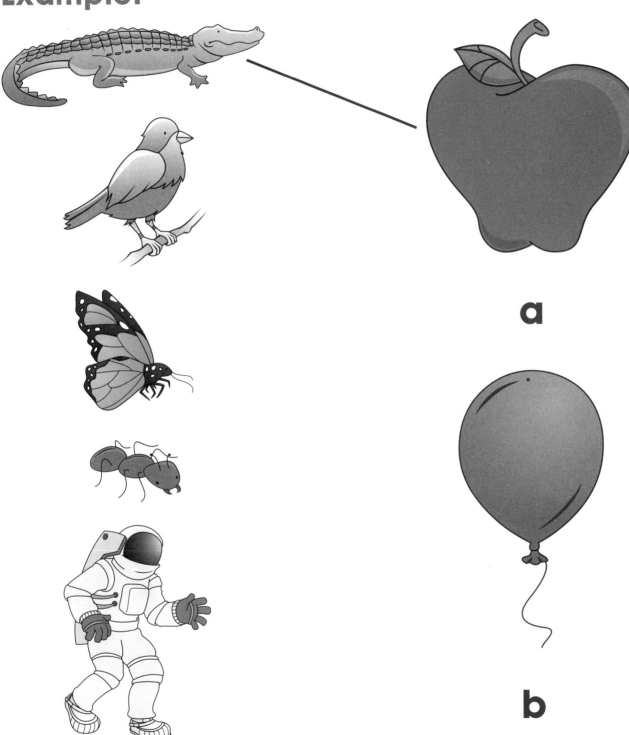

a

b

© Carson-Dellosa

DAY 14

Say the name of each picture. Draw a line from each little picture to the big picture that begins with the same sound.

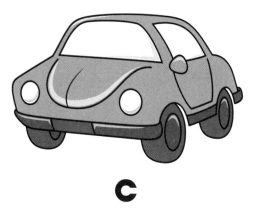

c

d

© Carson-Dellosa

PLACE STICKER HERE

Say the name of each picture. Draw a line from each little picture to the big picture that begins with the same sound.

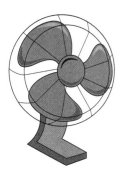

e

f

© Carson-Dellosa

DAY 15

Say the name of each picture. Circle the pictures that begin with the /g/ sound, like guitar.

g

Say the name of each picture. Circle the pictures that begin with the /h/ sound, like heart.

h

© Carson-Dellosa

PLACE
STICKER
HERE

Say the name of each picture. Circle the pictures that begin
with the /i/ sound, like igloo.

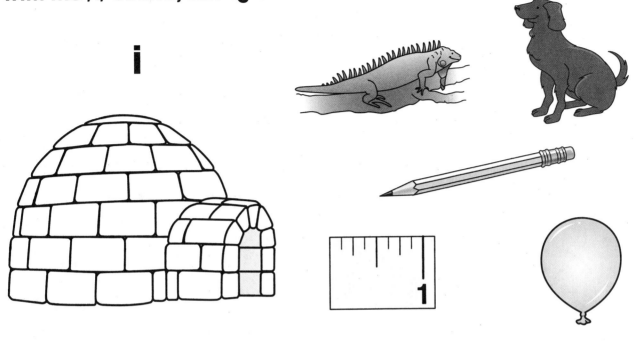

i

Say the name of each picture. Circle the pictures that begin
with the /j/ sound, like jar.

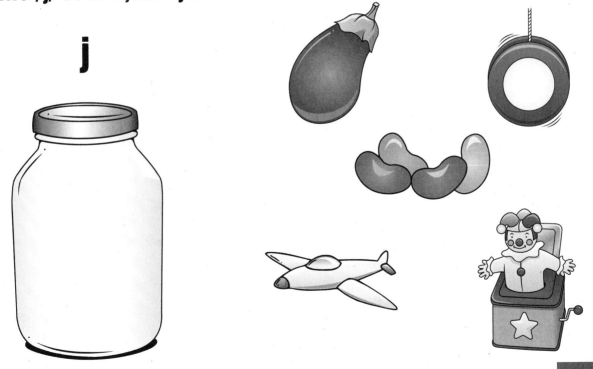

j

© Carson-Dellosa

DAY 16

Say the name of each picture. Circle the pictures that begin with the /k/ sound, like king.

k

Say the name of each picture. Circle the pictures that begin with the /l/ sound, like lion.

l

© Carson-Dellosa

PLACE STICKER HERE

Say the name of each picture. Circle the pictures that begin with the /m/ sound, like moon.

Say the name of each picture. Circle the pictures that begin with the /n/ sound, like nail.

© Carson-Dellosa

DAY 17

Say the name of each picture. Circle the pictures that begin with the /o/ sound, like ostrich.

o

Say the name of each picture. Circle the pictures that begin with the /p/ sound, like pumpkin.

p

© Carson-Dellosa

PLACE STICKER HERE

Say the name of each picture. Circle the pictures that have the letter *q*, like queen.

q

Say the name of each picture. Circle the pictures that begin with the /r/ sound, like rocket.

r

© Carson-Dellosa

DAY 18

Say the name of each picture. Draw a line from each little picture to the big picture that begins with the same sound.

s

t

© Carson-Dellosa

PLACE STICKER HERE

Say the name of each picture. Circle the pictures that begin with the /u/ sound, like umbrella.

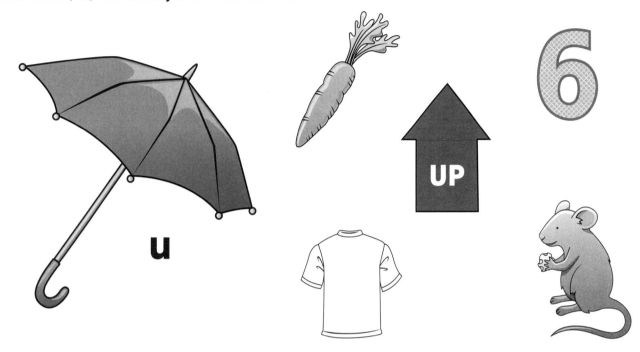

Say the name of each picture. Circle the pictures that begin with the /v/ sound, like vase.

© Carson-Dellosa

DAY 19

Say the name of each picture. Circle the pictures that begin with the /w/ sound, like window.

W

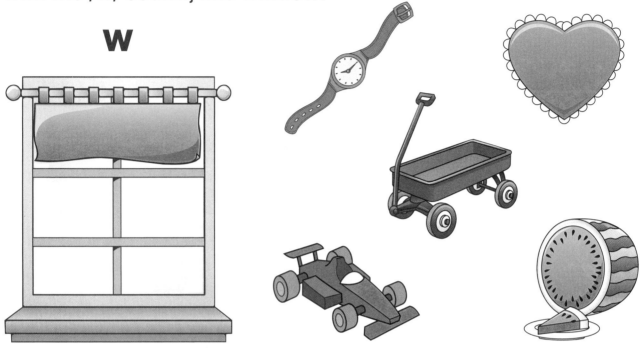

Say the name of each picture. Circle the pictures that have the letter *x*, like X-ray.

X

© Carson-Dellosa

PLACE STICKER HERE

Say the name of each picture. Circle the pictures that begin with the /y/ sound, like yak.

y

Say the name of each picture. Circle the pictures that begin with the /z/ sound, like zigzag.

z

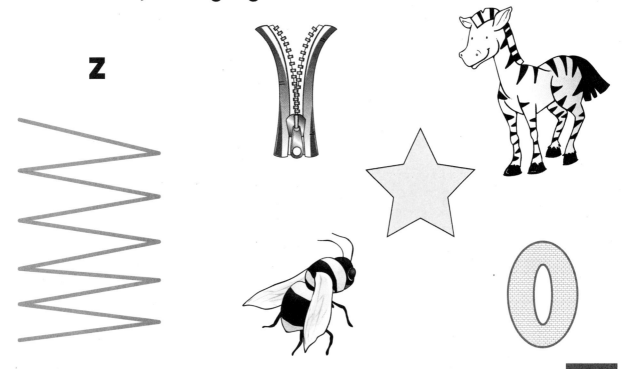

© Carson-Dellosa

DAY 20

Have an adult help you measure your height and weight again. Fill in the blanks. Compare these measurements to your measurements on page 3. Then, draw yourself below and color the picture.

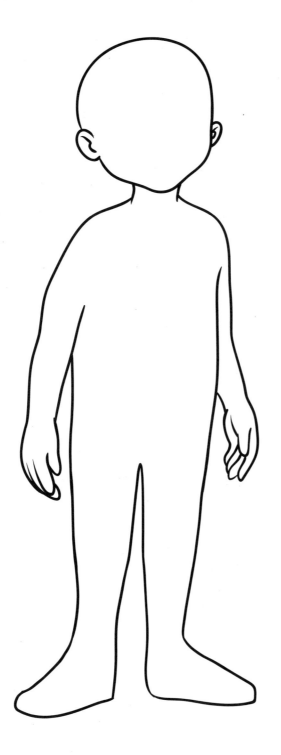

Your Height:

_____

Your Weight:

_____

PLACE STICKER HERE

© Carson-Dellosa

Sun and Shade

Do objects in the sun feel warmer than objects in the shade? Which colors absorb the most heat?

Materials:
- 2 sheets of black paper
- 2 sheets of white paper

Procedure:
Help your child place one sheet of black paper and one sheet of white paper in direct sunlight. Place one sheet of black paper and one sheet of white paper in complete shade. After one hour, touch each sheet of paper. Compare the paper in the sun with the paper in the shade. Ask your child the following questions.

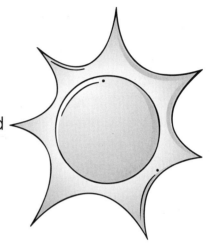

1. Which sheet of paper felt the warmest? _____

   _____

2. Which sheet of paper felt the coolest? _____

   _____

3. Why did one pair of papers feel warmer than the other pair? _____

   _____

4. What color shirt would keep you cooler on a sunny day? _____

   _____

© Carson-Dellosa

Jumping Jack Challenge

Provide your child with an opportunity to show his endurance level and to challenge yours. Select short, fun, upbeat songs. Turn on the music and start doing jumping jacks along with your child. See if you both can jump through the first song together.
Continue for a few songs and rest in between based on your and your child's stamina. If you find that jumping jacks are too challenging, simply jumping in place will also provide great exercise and an endurance challenge. Complete another jumping jack challenge each week. With each jumping jack session, incorporate longer songs and take fewer breaks to see how you both progress as your endurance improves.

Jump and Count

For this activity, you and your child will need the number flash cards at the back of this book and a jump rope.

Help your child shuffle the number flash cards and place them facedown on the ground. Flip over a number flash card. Your child should jump rope the number of times shown. Count your child's jumps aloud together. Once all of the cards have been flipped over, have your child arrange them in order from 0 to 12. Take turns jumping rope and flipping number flash cards until you have each completed the activity twice.

* See page ii.

© Carson-Dellosa

Yes, I Can!

Explain to your child that perseverance means refusing to give up. Ask your child to draw a picture of the hardest thing she has ever done. Once she has finished, invite her to share her picture with you and tell you the story. Then, post her picture in a visible location as a reminder to never give up.

Supporting Stories

Discuss with your child what it means to be loyal using examples to which he can relate, such as supporting and standing up for the people in his life. Invite your child to write a story about loyalty. Talk about an example of loyalty that he has seen or experienced. Remind him of recent events if needed. Talk about how to turn this into a story. Have him recall the order of events as you record them on paper. His story should have a beginning, a middle, and an end.

Provide him with craft materials to make a book cover. Bind the book with staples or punch holes along the book's spine and secure it with brass paper fasteners or yarn. Help him add a title that incorporates the idea of loyalty.

© Carson-Dellosa

Take It Outside!

Play a game of hopscotch to reinforce counting skills. Use sidewalk chalk to draw a basic, numbered hopscotch pattern on a safe sidewalk or driveway. Find two outdoor objects for you and your child to pick up, such as pinecones or smooth stones. To add counting and physical challenges, draw another hopscotch pattern with random numbers so that your child has to jump a little farther and find the numbers in order. Add more numbers as your child becomes familiar with each pattern.

Invite your child to a summer picnic! Make sandwiches, snacks, and drinks. Put it all in a picnic basket and grab a blanket. Before eating, talk about the five senses—taste, smell, sight, hearing, and touch. As your child eats each food item, talk about the variety of tastes and smells, such as the salty potato chips and sweet apple slices. Point out the things you and your child can hear, see, and feel during the picnic, like the crunch of the carrots, the color of the birds, and the softness of the grass beneath the blanket.

Explain to your child that when paper, plastic, metal, or glass is recycled, it is remade into something useful. For example, plastic milk jugs may become building materials. Recycled glass bottles or aluminum cans can be remade into new bottles or cans.

Talk about ways that recycling is good for the planet, such as conserving natural resources and saving landfill space. If your community participates in a recycling program, allow your child to help you sort the recyclable items or take a trip to the recycling center to drop off your recyclable materials.

* See page ii.

© Carson-Dellosa

Match each word to the correct picture.

Example:

sun

dog

bat

pin

hen

© Carson-Dellosa

Match each word to the correct picture.

gum

egg

nut

ant

log

© Carson-Dellosa

Circle the word in each row that names the picture.

 cap   van   rat

 tip   job   sun

 day   boy   bed

 on   ant   end

 bat   yak   fun

© Carson-Dellosa

BONUS

Circle the word in each row that names the picture.

	cat in mug
	am leg up
	mop bug dip
	mat net hit
	rag jet wig

© Carson-Dellosa

Trace and write the letters A–E.

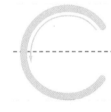

© Carson-Dellosa

BONUS

Trace and write the letters F–J.

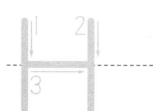

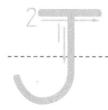

© Carson-Dellosa

Trace and write the letters K–O.

© Carson-Dellosa

BONUS

Trace and write the letters P–T.

© Carson-Dellosa

Trace and write the letters U–Y.

© Carson-Dellosa

BONUS

Trace and write the letter Z.

Z   z

Trace and write the numbers 0–5.

0   1

2   3

4   5

© Carson-Dellosa

Trace and write the numbers 6–10.

6

7

8

9

10

Practice writing your name.

© Carson-Dellosa

BONUS

Trace the letters.

A B C D E F

G H I J K L

M N O P Q

R S T U V W

X Y Z

© Carson-Dellosa

A B C

D E F

G H I

© Carson-Dellosa

c	b	a
© Carson-Dellosa	© Carson-Dellosa	© Carson-Dellosa
f	e	d
© Carson-Dellosa	© Carson-Dellosa	© Carson-Dellosa
i	h	g
© Carson-Dellosa	© Carson-Dellosa	© Carson-Dellosa

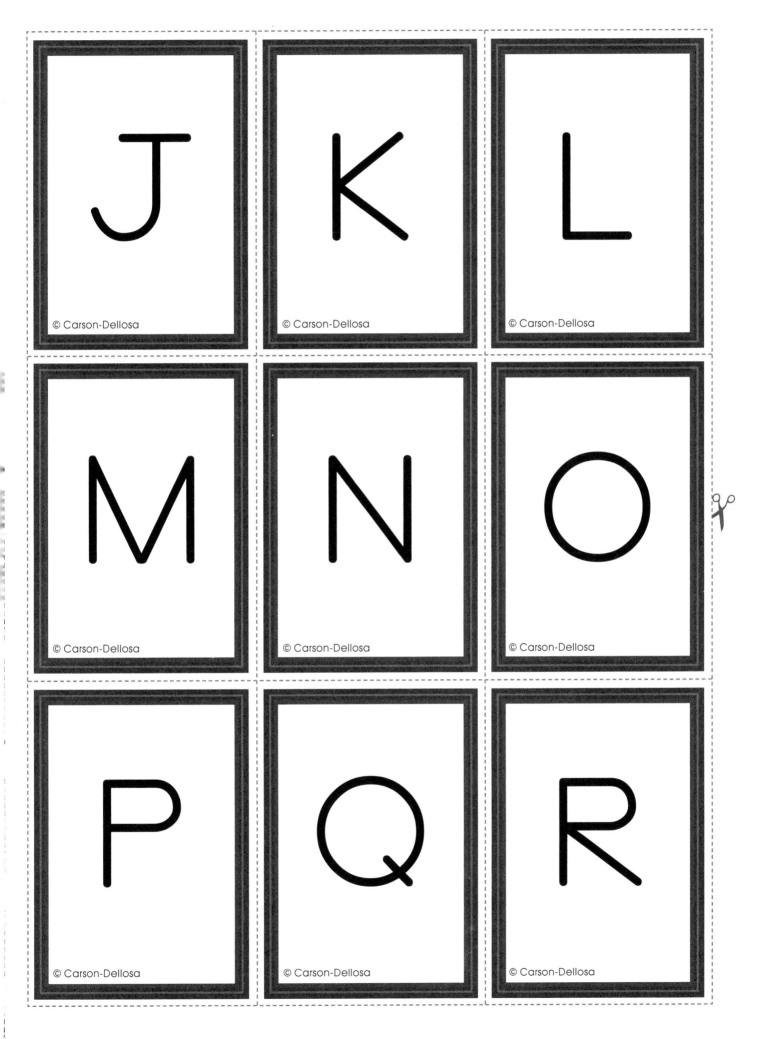

J

K

L

© Carson-Dellosa

© Carson-Dellosa

© Carson-Dellosa

M

N

O

© Carson-Dellosa

© Carson-Dellosa

© Carson-Dellosa

P

Q

R

© Carson-Dellosa

© Carson-Dellosa

© Carson-Dellosa

l

© Carson-Dellosa

k

© Carson-Dellosa

j

© Carson-Dellosa

o

© Carson-Dellosa

n

© Carson-Dellosa

m

© Carson-Dellosa

r

© Carson-Dellosa

q

© Carson-Dellosa

p

© Carson-Dellosa

S	T	U
© Carson-Dellosa	© Carson-Dellosa	© Carson-Dellosa
V	W	X
© Carson-Dellosa	© Carson-Dellosa	© Carson-Dellosa
Y	Z	O
© Carson-Dellosa	© Carson-Dellosa	© Carson-Dellosa

u

© Carson-Dellosa

t

© Carson-Dellosa

s

© Carson-Dellosa

x

© Carson-Dellosa

w

© Carson-Dellosa

v

© Carson-Dellosa

© Carson-Dellosa

z

© Carson-Dellosa

y

© Carson-Dellosa

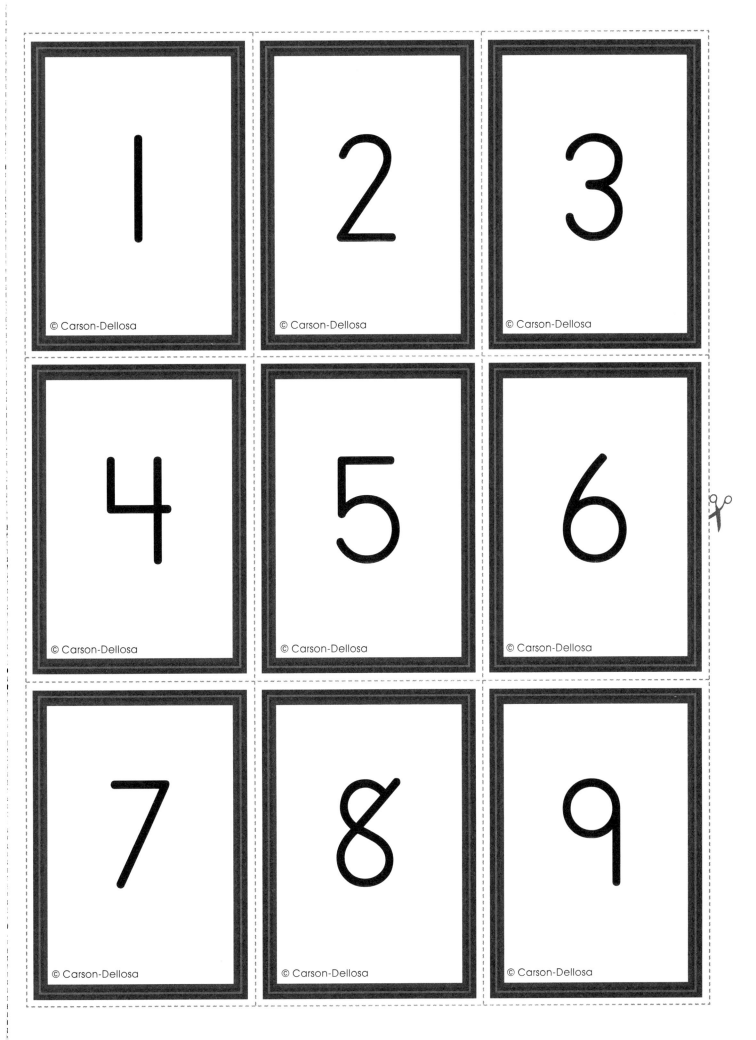

1   2   3

4   5   6

7   8   9

© Carson-Dellosa

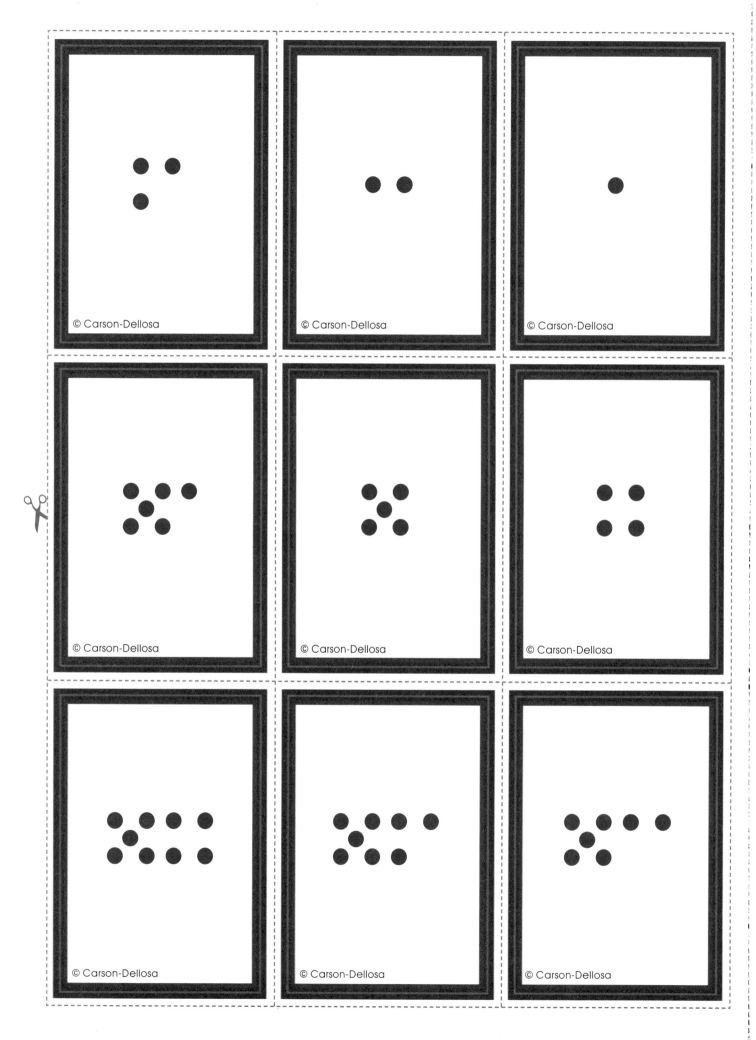

© Carson-Dellosa

© Carson-Dellosa

© Carson-Dellosa

© Carson-Dellosa

© Carson-Dellosa

© Carson-Dellosa

© Carson-Dellosa

© Carson-Dellosa

© Carson-Dellosa

10

© Carson-Dellosa

11

© Carson-Dellosa

12

© Carson-Dellosa

square

© Carson-Dellosa

circle

© Carson-Dellosa

triangle

© Carson-Dellosa

rectangle

© Carson-Dellosa

rhombus

© Carson-Dellosa

oval

© Carson-Dellosa

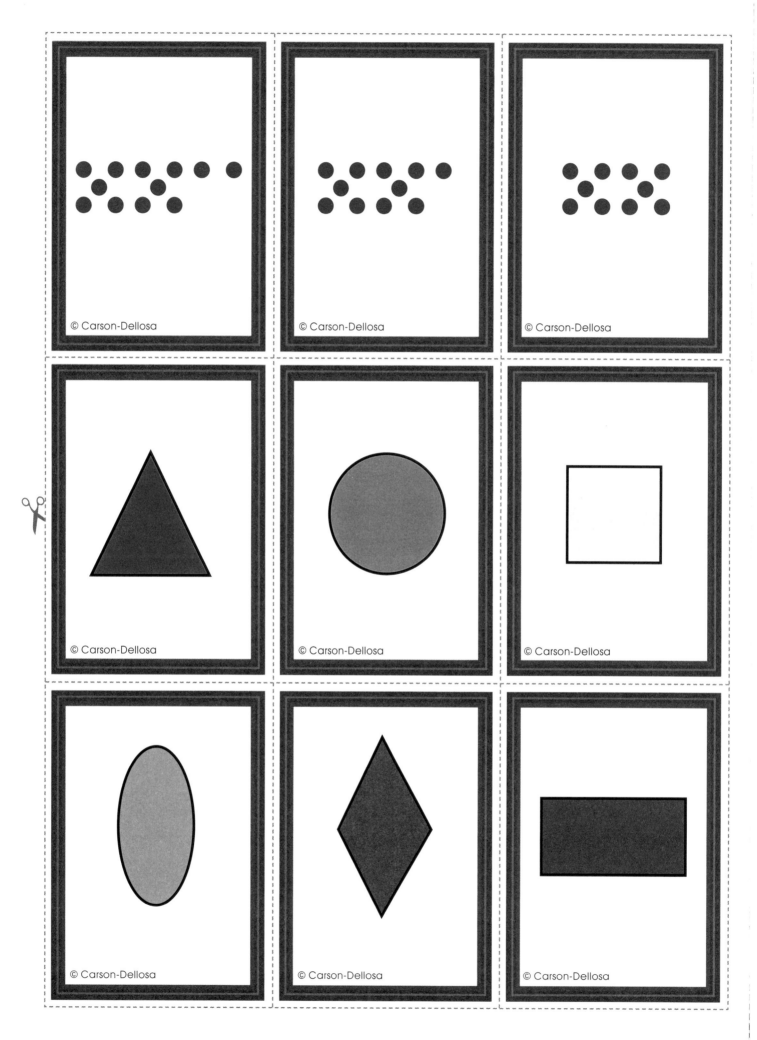

© Carson-Dellosa

© Carson-Dellosa

© Carson-Dellosa

© Carson-Dellosa

© Carson-Dellosa

© Carson-Dellosa

© Carson-Dellosa

© Carson-Dellosa

© Carson-Dellosa

red	orange	yellow
© Carson-Dellosa	© Carson-Dellosa	© Carson-Dellosa
green	blue	purple
© Carson-Dellosa	© Carson-Dellosa	© Carson-Dellosa
black	brown	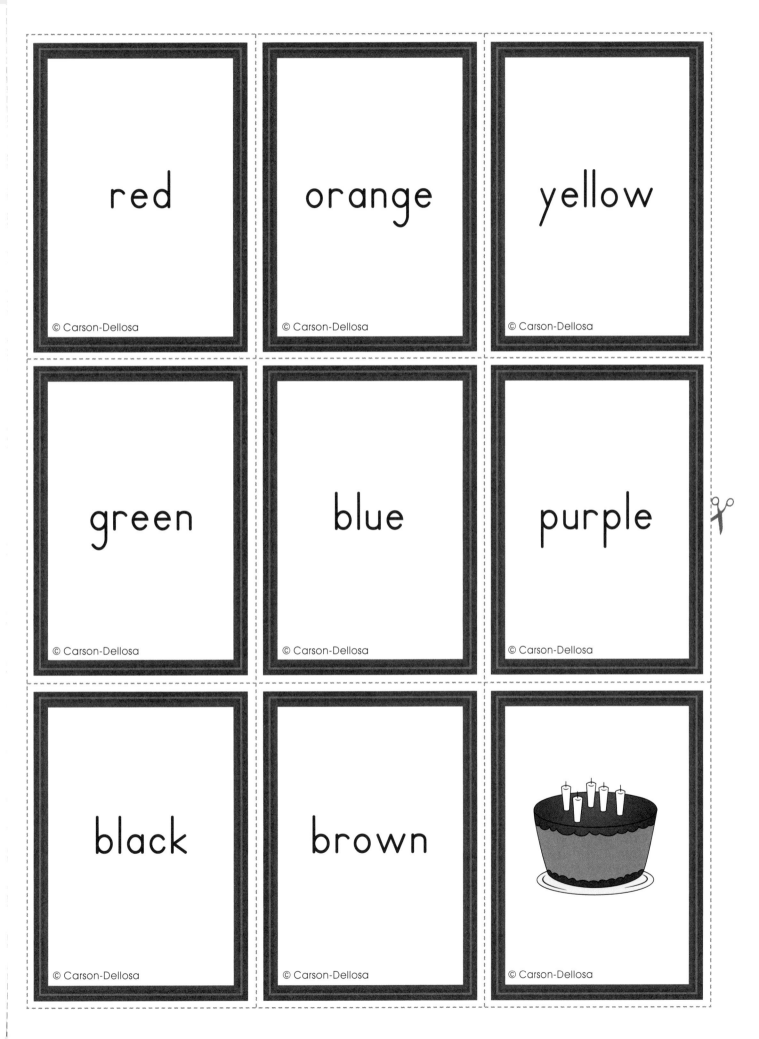
© Carson-Dellosa	© Carson-Dellosa	© Carson-Dellosa

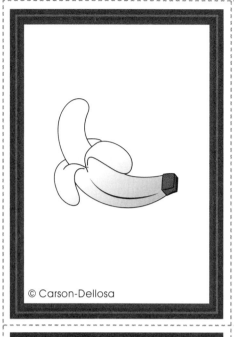

© Carson-Dellosa

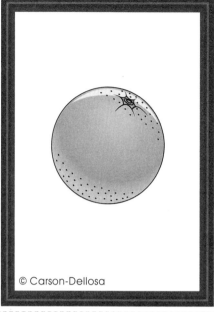

© Carson-Dellosa

© Carson-Dellosa

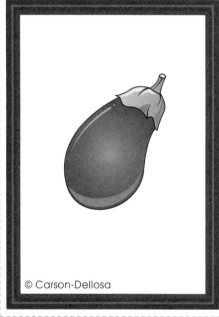

© Carson-Dellosa

© Carson-Dellosa

© Carson-Dellosa

© Carson-Dellosa

© Carson-Dellosa

© Carson-Dellosa

The Original
Summer Bridge Activities™

Congratulations!

This certifies that

_____
Name

has completed **Summer Bridge Activities** ™.

_____
Parent's Signature

www.carsondellosa.com